THE SPIRIT OF
GALLIPOLI

The Spirit of
GALLIPOLI

The birth of the Anzac legend

PATRICK LINDSAY

Hardie Grant Books

Published in Australia in 2013
by Hardie Grant Books

Hardie Grant Books (Australia)
Ground Floor, Building 1
658 Church Street
Richmond, Victoria 3121
www.hardiegrant.com.au

Hardie Grant Books (UK)
Dudley House, North Suite
34–35 Southampton Street
London WC2E 7HF
www.hardiegrant.co.uk

Cataloguing-in-Publication data is available from the
National Library of Australia.

ISBN 9781742706146

Front cover photographs courtesy
Australian War Memorial (AWM G00599) and Getty Images
Back cover photograph courtesy the author
Cover and internal design by Gayna Murphy, Greendot Design
Typesetting by Kirby Jones
Printed and bound in China by C&C Offset Printing

CONTENTS

�֎

Dedicated to the Anzacs
and the men of Turkey who faced them

For Lisa, Nathan, Kate and Sarah

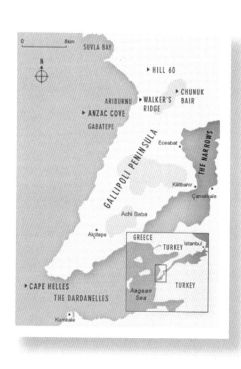

Introduction

The battlefields of the Gallipoli Peninsula in western Turkey possess a special aura. Australians and New Zealanders who travel halfway around the world to visit them are invariably struck as soon as they arrive. They feel an affinity with the souls of their forebears who rest there and a deep respect for the Turkish defenders who stood opposite them.

The Gallipoli campaign involved many countries but it had an especially powerful and lasting impact on three in particular: Turkey, Australia and New Zealand. Each was a fledgling nation at the time: Australia and New Zealand were only recently independent from the British Empire, and Turkey was still emerging from the Ottoman Empire.

For each, the Gallipoli campaign was a crusade and, at the same time, a national rite of passage; all three countries emerged with enhanced international reputations, and each saw its image clarified in its national consciousness. Not surprisingly, each now regards the calamitous events of 1915 as a coming of age in its growth to maturity.

The tragic irony of the campaign is that, handled properly, it could have been a relatively 'clean' triumph for the Allies. Alas, in the end, it ranks as one of the bloodiest military engagements in history, where two armies, each of around a half a million men, fought to a standstill. Each side lost approximately half its strength in casualties.

PATRICK LINDSAY

Ari Burnu Cemetery, overlooking Anzac Cove, where some of the first Anzacs to fall on Gallipoli are buried.

What began as a superpower flexing its muscles against an archaic Asian 'Dad's Army', ended as a prequel to another Asian war half-a-century later. The lessons were not learned: the result was the same.

In 1985 at Ari Burnu Cemetery at the northern end of the Gallipoli Peninsula, the Turkish Government unveiled a monument and officially named the place *Anzac Koyu*, or Anzac Cove.

The monument immortalises the words of Mustafa Kemal, one of the commanders who fought against the Anzacs and who went on, as Kemal Ataturk, to become the first president of his nation. Addressing Anzac and British veterans and their families in 1934, Kemal Ataturk said:

> 'Those heroes that shed their blood and lost their lives ... you are now lying in the soil of a friendly country. Therefore rest in peace, there is no difference between the Johnnies and Mehmets to us where they lie side by side here in this country of ours ... You the mothers, who sent their sons from far away countries, wipe away your tears; your sons are now living in our bosom and are in peace.

PATRICK LINDSAY

The memorial at Ari Burnu immortalising Ataturk's speech of reconciliation.

After having lost their lives on this land they have become our sons as well.'

Could there be a more generous sentiment of forgiveness and humanity from one warrior to his foes?

There have been many historical revisions of the Gallipoli campaign but, as with most momentous events, those who were there speak with the greatest authority. Wherever possible, I've tried to use their own personal accounts in telling their story.

Patrick Lindsay, 2006

CHAPTER ONE

The Road to War

Throughout the 19th century, Europe dominated the world stage. By the dawn of the 20th, one country in particular had emerged as an aggressive maverick and a showdown – of some description – seemed almost inevitable.

Between 1800 and 1914 European powers, through their colonies or former colonies, extended their footprint on the earth's surface from 35 per cent to 84 per cent, as the railway, the telegraph and the steamship opened the way for the first stages of what we now know as globalisation.

During this period, the world endured many armed conflicts. Most, thankfully, were contained: the Taiping Rebellion in China in 1850–64; the Crimean War in 1854–56; the Italian War of 1859; the US Civil War in 1861–65; the Seven Weeks' War in 1866; the Franco–Prussian War in 1870–71; and the Russo–Turkish War in 1877–78.

AWM H12326

Germany's Kaiser studying maps with Marshall von Hindenberg and General Ludendorff.

In 1871, Germany unified as a nation and her new-found nationalism quickly became apparent. In 1879 she signed an alliance with Austria rather than Russia, which upset the delicate international balance and prompted Germany's neighbours – France on the west and Russia on the east – to sign a protective alliance a few years later.

In 1898, Germany caused further concern, particularly in Britain, by overtly strengthening her navy. The threat moved Britain to change her policy of avoiding alliances and, in 1904, she signed the *Entente Cordiale* (or 'friendly relations' agreement) with France. Three years later, Britain created the Triple Entente when she allied herself with her other major colonial rival, Russia.

Battlelines were being drawn, Europe was effectively divided into two armed camps, and citizens on both sides soon began to see conflict as not merely inevitable but as welcome.

By the summer of 1914 the political climate had deteriorated to the point where a single pistol shot was all that was required to ignite a firestorm. On 28 June, in Sarajevo, a 19-year-old Serbian nationalist, Gavrilo Princip, assassinated Archduke Franz Ferdinand, the heir to the Emperor of Austria–Hungary.

Austria–Hungary suspected Serbia was behind the killing, demanded an immediate investigation and threatened war.

Germany secretly backed Austria–Hungary, giving it 'blank cheque' support.

Russia supported Serbia.

Although Serbia accepted almost all the demands made of her, Austria–Hungary declared war on Serbia on 28 July 1914. Two days later Russia mobilised her armed forces. Germany insisted that she stop. France mobilised on 2 August and Germany demanded access through Belgium to take action. Britain demanded Germany stop. Germany ignored Britain's call.

By 4 August 1914, Britain, France and Russia were officially at war. The first 'shot' was a single, harmless round loosed by gunners at Port Nepean at the entrance to Melbourne's Port Phillip Bay. The soldiers were trying to prevent the German freighter *Pfalz* from fleeing the bay; it was just hours after they had heard of the declaration of war.

As loyal members of the British Empire, Australia and New Zealand followed Britain's lead and declared war on Germany immediately, at 9 am Sydney time on 5 August 1914.

New Zealand offered a contingent of troops; Canada offered 20,000 men; and the Australian Prime Minister, Joseph Cook, followed, offering an initial force of 20,000 and the Royal Australian Navy. Both would be available for service anywhere in the world.

At the time Australia was embroiled in a bitter Federal election – only its sixth since Federation in 1901. Parliament had been dissolved on 27 June and a poll was set for 5 September.

Speaking at Horsham in Victoria on 31 July, Australia's Prime Minister had said: 'If there is to be a war, you and I shall be in it. We must be in it. If the old country is at war, so are we.'

Australia's opposition Labor Leader, Andrew Fisher, was of a similar mind, and announced at Colac in Victoria the same night:

> 'Should the worst happen, after everything has been done that honour will permit, Australians will stand beside the mother country to help and defend her to our last man and our last shilling.'

This level of support was not surprising – the Australian and New Zealand people in those days were made up of principally English, Irish, Scottish and Welsh stock. New Zealand Maori and Pacific Islanders accounted for only 12 per cent of New Zealand's population and the Australian Aborigines only about 1 per cent of Australia's. Both countries were still deeply imbued with all things British – culture, literature, sport, commerce, government and royalty. In fact, Australia's disparate states and territories had only joined to form an independent nation 13 years earlier; while New Zealand had been independent for just seven.

In spite of their short histories of nationhood, Australians and New Zealanders had each developed a strength of character and a fierce independence which would serve them well in the conflicts ahead.

❧

Within days of the declaration of war, Australia and New Zealand began recruiting volunteers for the forces they had promised Britain: the Australian Imperial Force (AIF) and the New Zealand Expeditionary Force (NZEF).

Men came from every corner to join up. Many were from rural areas and it was a matter of great pride in their districts that they be accepted. In those days, recruiters were very particular and the medical examinations were tough. They often rejected men with defective or false teeth. (Within a year, the medicos had eased this restriction.) Australian recruits had to be at least 5' 6" tall, have a chest measurement of at least 34 inches and be aged between 19 and 38.

Many were given heroes' send-offs from their towns and couldn't face returning home with the shame of being rejected. World War I correspondent, Charles Bean, tells of one young Melburnian who was knocked back four times before finally getting the nod in Sydney; and another who rode more than 600 kilometres to Melbourne, where he was rejected, before catching a train to enlist in Adelaide. He was knocked back there too so he travelled on to Hobart without luck before finally being accepted in Sydney.

AWM ARTV00433

AWM ARTV001149

Top: Poster used to promote recruitment, playing on the consequences of not being part of the action.

Left: Recruitment poster, appealing to fear for family and patriotism.

AWM ARTV00142

Recruitment poster, appealing to mateship as wounded soldier looks into distance for reinforcements.

When the AIF detachment was complete, about a third of the infantry and a quarter of the light horse brigade consisted of civilians with no military experience. The rest were drawn from the regular army (including some from the British Army) and from the militia (the equivalent of today's Army Reserve).

The Australian plan was for New South Wales and Victoria to each provide a brigade of 4000 infantrymen in four battalions of 1000 — the 1st to 4th Battalions coming from New South Wales and the 5th to 8th from Victoria. Queensland would create the 9th Battalion; South Australia the 10th; Western Australia the 11th; and the 12th would come from a combination of Tasmania, Western Australia and South Australia.

The New Zealanders formed battalions from Auckland, Canterbury, Wellington and Otago.

The Australian Parliament decided private soldiers would receive the same wage as the average worker: six shillings a day. New Zealand soldiers would receive five shillings a day. The American private was on the equivalent of four shillings and seven pence a day, while the British infantryman received just one shilling a day. The Australians would soon earn the nickname 'the six-bob-a-day tourists'.

But money wasn't the lure that saw young men rushing the recruitment offices. It was the promise of the adventure of a lifetime tinged with the fear of 'not being in it'. The most pessimistic observers foresaw a conflict that might last a few months, perhaps a year, at worst.

Cecil Malthus spoke for many when he described his feelings as he enlisted in the 1st Canterbury Battalion in Nelson at the northern tip of New Zealand's South Island:

> 'The prospect of seeing service gave us a thrill of pure joy, and indeed the feeling throughout New Zealand was mainly one of pleasurable excitement.'

CHAPTER TWO

The Storm Breaks

While young Australians and New Zealanders rushed to enlist, war exploded across Europe.

In the first week of hostilities, the Germans attacked Belgium, the French moved on Alsace and the Russians advanced into East Prussia.

On 22 August 1914 the British Expeditionary Force arrived in France but was soon forced back by the Germans to a line along the Marne River, the natural barrier between the invaders and Paris.

By 9 September the Germans realised they had overreached themselves and withdrew to positions along the Aisne River and its tributaries where they dug in. This was to be the start of years of trench warfare – a devastatingly wasteful war of attrition.

By the first battle for Ypres, in Belgium – a mere four months into the conflict – the French had suffered half a million casualties, including 300,000 killed, out of a male population of some 20 million. In the

AWM E00842

Part of the 760 kilometres of trenches which scarred the Western Front
battlefields.

same period Germany suffered 240,000 casualties from a male population of 32 million. Britain and Belgium lost approximately 30,000 men each.

The Western Front formed an ugly scar across Europe – a continuous line of trenches that ran 760 kilometres from the North Sea to the Swiss Alps.

In the East, the Germans were initially buoyed by a decisive victory in the battle of Tannenberg in late August where they surrounded and defeated two Russian armies and took 92,000 prisoners.

But a stalemate soon ensued.

When war was declared, Britain had asked Australia to seize Germany's New Guinea colony, and the Australian Naval and Military Expeditionary Force, a joint army–navy contingent, duly sailed for the capital, Rabaul, on New Britain Island. There, while capturing a German radio station at Bitapaka on 11 September 1914, Australia suffered her first casualties.

Able Seaman WGV Williams, a Melbourne City Council employee from Northcote, was fatally wounded – the first Australian to die on active service.

In all, Australia lost two officers and four soldiers, while one other officer and three men were wounded.

The Germans lost one non-commissioned officer and 30 native soldiers.

By the end of August, the AIF had 881 officers and 19,745 men of other ranks ready for action. Kitted out in their khaki serge uniforms and slouch hats, they sailed from their various home States and gathered in Western Australia's Albany Harbour.

In New Zealand, the NZEF's 'Main Body' of 8417 men were also ready for action and, on 14 October, they set

The first troopships carrying Australian and New Zealand soldiers, horses and supplies, leaving Albany in 1914.

sail from Wellington. It was a remarkable commitment given New Zealand's population at the time was roughly one million (compared with Australia's five million and Canada's seven). In fact, the NZEF was the largest single body of men ever to leave the Land of the Long White Cloud. It rendezvoused with the AIF at Albany Harbour before both armies headed off in convoy on 1 November, bound – or so they thought – for South Africa and then Britain via the Cape of Good Hope.

In October 1914, Germany and Austria–Hungary combined forces to invade Russia. Russia declared

AWM A02875

Group portrait of all the original officers and men of the 11th Battalion, 3rd Brigade, AIF on a pyramid outside Cairo.

war on Turkey, who had joined the Central Powers on 5 November 1914, and in turn, Britain and France declared war on her.

Given these new developments, and the fact that there was no suitable winter accommodation available for such a large number of troops in Britain, the Australian and New Zealand soldiers were re-routed to Colombo in Ceylon (now Sri Lanka) on the way to Cairo in Egypt. It was here that the Australians and New Zealanders gained their first insight into the extent of the British Empire's involvement in the conflict.

While training at Mena Camp – in the shadow of the pyramids outside Cairo at the edge of the Libyan Desert – the young Australians and New Zealanders were placed under the command of 49-year-old General Sir William Birdwood, a British Indian Army officer and veteran of the Indian and African Wars.

Birdwood had originally proposed calling his corps the 'Australasian Army Corps'. Not surprisingly, the New Zealanders weren't impressed, and the name was swiftly changed to the Australian and New Zealand Army Corps.

The corps was to comprise two infantry divisions as well as a mounted division. The 1st Australian Division formed Birdwood's first group but he realised he had too few New Zealanders and too many Australians

AWM J00450

Men of the original Light Horse Regiment in training before leaving
Australia for Egypt and Gallipoli.

to maintain two separate groups, so he combined Brigadier Earl Johnson's New Zealand Brigade and the New Zealand Mounted Rifles Brigade with Australian units — Monash's 4th Brigade and Chauvel's Light Horse Brigade — to create what he called the New Zealand and Australian Division as his second group.

The famous 'Anzac' acronym was born around this time. The Australians credited it to Lieutenant AT White, one of Birdwood's staff. The New Zealanders claimed their Sergeant KM Little invented it for a rubber stamp for equipment. Either way, it was soon established as the force's telegraphic code name and in time became the proud collective noun for both the group and the individuals within it.

In Egypt, as the Australians and New Zealanders met and mixed with their counterparts from Britain and the other Commonwealth countries, it became clear to all that they were well above average in size compared with the other troops.

Charles Bean notes:

> 'Subsequently, many visitors from Great Britain and the Western Front declared that the Australians and New Zealanders in Egypt

AWM A05381

War correspondent and historian Charles Bean outside his tent at Mena Camp, Egypt in 1915.

and Gallipoli were the biggest men that they
had seen in any force.'

During training, the Anzacs established their reputation
as boisterous soldiers with a cavalier attitude towards
old-fashioned 'spit and polish' discipline. They drank
(often too much of the local brew) at the street cafés and
frequented many of the area's low establishments, and
indulged in assorted high jinks and pranks, including
on one occasion taking General Birdwood's staff car
for a joyride! Their refusal to salute British officers
became the accepted (if often resented) norm.

At one point New Zealand officers warned their
troops to steer clear of the troublesome Australians
and the Australian commanders resorted to sending a
few intractable offenders home.

New Zealand soldiers saw action in Egypt first, on
3 February 1915, when they repulsed a small Turkish
raid on the Suez Canal. Private William Ham of the
New Zealand Canterbury Infantry Regiment was badly
wounded and died the next day. He became the first
Anzac officially killed in action. The rest of the Anzac
force settled into training and manoeuvres in the
Sahara Desert and awaited orders.

The only other skirmish of note during this period involved a less-than-glorious riot that broke out on 2 April 1915 in Cairo's brothel district, the Haret el Wassa (known to the soldiers as 'the Wozzer').

Troops from Australian and New Zealand units reacted to what they felt were shady dealings by the district's inhabitants and what started as a local disturbance soon flared into a full-scale riot involving some 3000 men. At the height of the trouble, the troops tried to evict many of the Wozzer's ladies and pimps, throwing their furniture into the street and setting fire to it.

By the time order was restored three Aussies and a Kiwi were wounded by stray bullets from the military police and the Anzacs were hit with a hefty damage bill.

Clearly, the Anzacs were spoiling for a fight.

If only they knew what awaited them.

CHAPTER THREE

Breaking the Stalemate

Across Europe's Western Front, vast armies from both sides were now living in a putrid maze of trenches. They opposed one another across often narrow stretches of land that were known as no-man's-land.

Every time one side tried to break the deadlock by 'frontal' attacks they inevitably suffered massive losses. Nonetheless, they continued to launch repeated assaults against walls of barbed wire and machine-gun nests, squandering thousands of lives for a few metres of territory. Over the months, the armies dug more than 50,000 kilometres of trenches as they sank further into a muddy stalemate. The British Army alone used 10.6 million spades during the war!

Meanwhile, on the Eastern Front, Russia was faring poorly and sensed her problems would only increase after Turkey sided with Germany following a series of flirtations with both sides.

In the lead-up to the war, Britain had been building two state-of-the-art Dreadnought-class battleships for the Turkish Government, the *Reshadieh* and the *Sultan Osman I*. The *Sultan Osman I* contained more guns than any previous battleship and their delivery was eagerly anticipated in Turkey, not in the least because they'd been paid for by public subscription. They were to form the basis for a rejuvenated Turkish navy.

As war become imminent, the two battleships took on increased importance. Britain only had a narrow advantage over Germany in numbers of Dreadnoughts and the 39-year-old First Lord of the Admiralty, Winston Churchill, knew it would have been the height of folly to hand them over to Turkey if there were any chance they could be used against Britain. He ordered the boats' builders to detain them.

The Turks had anticipated Churchill's move and ordered the captain of the *Sultan Osman I* to take on fuel and to head for Constantinople even before the ship was completed. But the British security forces acted swiftly. They quarantined and boarded the vessels, thus preventing the Turks from raising their flag on them and claiming them as their own.

Britain advised the Turkish Government it would give 'all due consideration' to compensating Turkey for 'financial and other loss' following the action taken.

The Turks had been holding secret talks with the Germans about an alliance in the weeks before war broke out, as they feared an Allied victory would see the break up of the last vestiges of the Ottoman Empire. They hoped that a German victory would help them recover their traditional lands in central Asia as well as the Caucasus, which they had lost in the 1877–78 war with Russia.

The Germans were initially doubtful about Turkey's value as an ally and were reluctant to commit unless the Turks could show some real benefit to the German cause. The Turks played their trump card on 1 August 1914 when they offered to hand over the *Sultan Osman I*

AWM AO3547

Field Marshall Horatio
Herbert Kitchener.

– then the most powerful warship in the world. A recent revelation from the Ottoman archives shows that when the Turks made their offer, they knew the ship had already been impounded by Britain!

Turkey's entry into the war had an immediate impact: it blocked Russia's only ice-free sea passage to the west through the Straits of the Dardanelles, the waterway linking the Black Sea to the Mediterranean, which Turkey controlled. Half of Russia's exports moved through this waterway and its closure stopped much-needed supplies and ammunition reaching Russia's Black Sea ports.

AWM H12243

Winston Churchill (centre, wearing a top hat) with members of the British Army Council.

Russia called for help from Britain to attack Turkey to ease the pressure on its own forces in the Caucasus. Britain's Secretary of State for War, the irascible former British Proconsul in Egypt, Field Marshall Horatio Herbert Kitchener (recently elevated to Earl Kitchener of Khartoum), was concerned by Russia's attitude. He feared that without Britain's help Russia may be forced out of the conflict, leaving France and Britain exposed to the full might of Germany's forces.

Searching for alternatives, the British conceived a radical plan: Winston Churchill proposed an assault on Turkey's capital, Constantinople (modern-day Istanbul), suggesting a successful attack would solve many problems: it would open the desired ice-free sea passage to Russia; take Germany's newest ally, Turkey, out of the war; and secure the Suez Canal. Churchill believed it could also persuade the as-yet-unaligned Balkan nations to support an Allied advance from the south against Germany and Austria–Hungary.

Churchill's plan was based on two key assumptions: firstly, that the fleet would easily overcome Turkish guns along the Gallipoli Peninsula at the entrance to the Dardanelles; and secondly, that Turkey would quickly surrender once British warships threatened her capital.

Churchill initially proposed a naval attack supported by land forces, but Lord Kitchener refused to release troops from the Western Front, so he had to be satisfied with a naval assault alone. He intended to use outdated British and French battleships to force their way through the straits of the Dardanelles, allowing the fleet to sail up the Sea of Marmara and bombard Constantinople at the gateway to the Black Sea.

The die was cast. With Lord Kitchener's concurrence, the civilian members of the Cabinet supported the plan and Churchill got his way.

CHAPTER FOUR

The Ottoman Prize

The land that Churchill planned to conquer had been fought over repeatedly since the Stone Age. Mediterranean peoples settled in Turkey around 7500 BC; the Hittites moved in during the Bronze Age; and about 1000 BC, when the biblical Kings Solomon and David held sway in Jerusalem, the first settlement, Semistra, was built on the site of modern-day Istanbul.

In 657 BC, a Greek colonist named Byzas followed the Delphic Oracle's advice and settled around Istanbul's natural harbour, the Golden Horn, and Byzantium was born.

Byzantium's position – on the western side of the land bridge which joins Europe and Asia and at the mouth of the waterway which runs from the Black Sea to the Sea of Marmara – made it one of the most strategically important gateways in the world. It was captured by the Persian emperor Darius in 512 BC, surrendered to Alexander the Great in 334 BC, overrun by the Kingdom of Pergamum in 179 BC and willed to the Roman Empire in 133 BC.

For a time, Byzantium prospered under the Romans, but it was razed after backing the loser in a civil war and only rose again when Constantine became emperor and built his new capital on the old site. He called it New Rome. That name didn't stick but Constantinople did and it soon became the undisputed Eurasian capital.

Constantine's successor, Theodosius, extended the city and built more massive walls to protect it from Attila and his Huns. His walls can still be seen today. He and the next Emperor, Justinian, also built the magnificent cathedral, the Aya Sofya (or Church of the Divine Wisdom) – the finest church in Christendom for almost a millennium and to this day a magnet for tourists from around the world.

The city's internal politics were so devious and convoluted they gave rise to the word 'Byzantine' which the Oxford Concise Dictionary describes as, '(of a political situation etc): extremely complicated, inflexible, carried on by underhand methods'. This could well have described both sides' operations during the World War I Gallipoli campaign. Ultimately, Byzantium became embroiled in the last Crusade and was destroyed in 1204. But, as always, it bounced back.

✹

From around 1000 AD the Ottoman Empire had begun to develop after invasions by nomadic Mongolian and Turkish-speaking horsemen from central and north-eastern Asia, like Tamerlane and Genghis Khan. It was originally called the Osmanli Empire after Osman (a *ghazi* or warrior for the Moslem faith born in the 13th century who fought against the Byzantine Empire in Anatolia). By the 15th century Osman's descendants had replaced the Byzantine Empire and Sultan Mehmet II created a unified Ottoman Empire when he conquered Constantinople in 1452.

But, even then, the Empire was so diverse that it is hard to imagine it as an 'empire' in the British sense of the word. The Ottoman states were remarkably varied — in national background, ethnic make-up, language, even religion — along with Turkey, they included Greece, the Balkans, Romania, Hungary, the Crimea, Iraq, Syria, Palestine, Egypt, Arabia and Libya.

The essential failing of the empire was that it was created, grew and was sustained by conquest. It never succeeded in mastering the art of government. When those it had conquered began to fight back and defeat the Ottomans during the 16th and 17th centuries, the ensuing internal pressures took a heavy toll. By 1875 the Empire was bankrupt.

It had a constitution briefly in 1876, under Sultan Abdul Hamid II, but he abolished it a year later and restored himself to absolute power. He held control until the so-called Young Turks rose in 1907.

Officially known as the Committee of Union and Progress, the Young Turks were a mix of young army and naval officers, academics and liberal reformers. They sounded gentle enough but they were deadly serious in their aims of forcing changes to the political structure. Members were even made to swear they would assassinate anyone that the group voted to eliminate. After a series of small uprisings and further threats of violent revolution, Abdul Hamid gave in and restored the constitution originally established in 1876. The following year the Young Turks deposed him and became the dominant political party.

In the build-up to World War I, the crumbling Ottoman Empire endured two Balkan Wars, in 1912 and 1913. During the first, the Bulgarians defeated the 1st Turkish Army and pushed it back to the Catalca Lines, only 30 kilometres from Constantinople. By November 1912 the 2nd Turkish Army was beaten by the Serbs and the Montenegrins and withdrew into

Albania. The Greeks took advantage of the situation, pushed north and took Salonika on 8 November.

By mid-December 1912 the warring parties were in London negotiating a peace treaty. Fearing the Grand Vizier would give away too much at the peace table, the Young Turks forced him to resign at gunpoint. Their insistence on retaining Adrianople (modern-day Edirne) broke up the talks.

The Bulgarians resumed their attacks and took Adrianople in March 1913. Then it was back to the negotiating table once again. The result was the Treaty of London, under which the Turks lost the Balkan lands that the Empire had held since the 15th century, including Adrianople.

The Second Balkan War erupted in June 1913 when Bulgaria broke with its allies and tried to grab Salonika. Its former allies, Romania and Montenegro, banded together to fight the Bulgarians who were forced to withdraw forces from Adrianople. Ever the opportunists, the Young Turks seized the moment and regained Adrianople in July.

That war ended with the Treaty of Bucharest in August 1913 under which Serbia doubled in size, Greece gained Salonika and much of Macedonia, Bulgaria acquired a small access to the Aegean Sea and the Ottoman Empire lost its long-held grip on the Balkans.

The two wars devastated the Turkish Army. Casualties exceeded a quarter of a million men and the conflicts destroyed 14 of the nation's 43 infantry divisions.

The men behind the Young Turks now held the crucial positions of power in the Turkish administration: Sait Halam was Prime Minister and Grand Vizier; Talat Pasha (*Pasha* means General) was Minister for the Interior; Enver Pasha was Minister for War; and Cemal Pasha was Minister of the Marine. These were the leaders largely responsible for Turkey's entry into World War I at Germany's side.

One other Turkish leader, who would play a key role in Turkey's history – both as the saviour of Gallipoli

Mustafa Kemal Bey (later Ataturk) (fourth from left) with some of his officers and staff.

and later as the first President of a democratic Turkey – was temporarily pushed aside after he clashed with Enver Pasha.

A 32-year-old Lieutenant Colonel named Mustafa Kemal was exiled from the centre of power and put out to pasture as the military attaché in Sofia. But fate would cast him as a vital player in the drama that was about to unfold.

CHAPTER FIVE

The Guns of March 18

Winston Churchill and the British Navy were confident they could break through the Dardanelles Straits and sail right up to Constantinople. They were convinced the Turks had no heart for a prolonged fight and would throw their hands up once faced with the might of the British Fleet.

The plan sounded simple enough but, before they could threaten the Turkish capital, the British first had to force their way through the Dardanelles – a stretch of water 60 kilometres long and between 1.5 and 6 kilometres wide – known in ancient times as the Hellespont.

The traditional crossing point of the Dardanelles is the Narrows, where the two shores are just 1500 metres apart. Here, in 480 BC, Persia's King Xerxes built a bridge of boats so his troops could cross on their way to invade Greece. In 334 BC, Alexander the Great travelled the other way, from Greece to invade Persia.

It was near the Narrows, on 19 February 1915, that a fleet, led by British Vice-Admiral Sackville Carden and including the super-Dreadnought *Queen Elizabeth*, began bombarding the Turkish positions.

Using their superior firepower, the British systemically shelled the Turks from outside the range of the Turkish guns. But they could not silence the Turkish batteries and were forced to withdraw.

Historians have argued that the Turkish defenders were running out of munitions and that had the British shown more determination, victory could have been theirs. But recent examinations of the Turkish archives by historian Harvey Broadbent have revealed that the defenders did have sufficient guns and troops to continue their fight.

The defenders also had history on their side. Since the middle of the 15th century, the Narrows had been guarded by the twin fortresses of Cimenlik on the Asian part and Kilitbahir on the Gallipoli Peninsula – built by the conqueror of Constantinople, Mehmet II.

Cimenlik (meaning 'grassy', because it's partly hidden by earthworks) protects the city of Canakkale. Kilitbahir means 'Lock of the Sea' and it guards the town of Eceabat. Mehmet II equipped each fort with massive cannons that effectively covered the

PATRICK LINDSAY

Some of the concealed ammunition dumps which supplied the Turkish gunners defending the Narrows.

PATRICK LINDSAY

Inside one of the heavily-protected ammunition stores defending the Narrows.

Kilitbahir Fortress guarding the European side of the Narrows.

The hills of Gallipoli overlooking the Narrows today which show the image of a Turkish soldier made from white stones, with words which translate as 'Traveller, halt! The soil you tread once witnessed the end of a generation. Listen in this quiet mound there once beat the heart of a nation.'

Narrows against attack by sea. Invading vessels have always had to run a deadly gauntlet.

In 1915, the modern Turkish guns were well manned and well concealed. In addition, the defenders had two critical natural advantages: the terrain and the powerful tides of the Dardanelles. The steep slopes and hills of the Gallipoli Peninsula and the Asian shoreline gave them cover and height. The constant five- or six-knot surface current, running down the straits into the face of the British ships, would also prove critical.

Well aware the British were coming via the sea, the Turks worked feverishly to strengthen their defences and to mine the waters through which the attackers would have to travel.

Strangely, the British elected to use civilian trawlers and other vessels as minesweepers. Their crews were inexperienced and unwilling to operate under fire. This was understandable given the powerful currents against them meant their pace was slow and they became sitting ducks for the Turkish guns. In the end they were regularly driven off before they could sweep clear the waters leading to the Narrows.

The Allied commanders were now in a quandary: they couldn't crush the Turkish guns unless they came in close enough to bring their massive firepower to bear, but they couldn't be sure that the mines had been

PATRICK LINDSAY

The type of Turkish mine which crippled the British Fleet on 18 March 1915.

cleared so that it was safe for them to venture in that close.

Following a last-minute change in command after Admiral Carden suffered a breakdown, Rear-Admiral John de Robeck led the Allied fleet – 18 battleships in all, including four French ships – back to attack the Turks on 18 March.

After some early successes against the shore batteries, the attackers' worst fears became reality. The Turks had secretly laid a line of mines parallel to the Asian shoreline a week before the attack. (The minelayer responsible, *Nusrat*, is today proudly on display at Canakkale's military museum, along with examples of the mines that turned the course of the campaign.)

Just when de Robeck may have entertained thoughts of victory, the ageing French cruiser *Bouvet* struck one of the *Nusrat*'s mines while reversing and sank, losing almost all her crew.

In quick succession, the British warships, *Irresistible* and *Ocean*, also struck mines and were both disabled and eventually sank. Many other ships were hit by the relentless Turkish artillery. In total, one third of the fleet was sunk or disabled on that day.

PATRICK LINDSAY

The minelayer *Nusrat* which secretly laid the mines which devastated the British Fleet on 18 March 1915, now on display in the Canakkale Military Museum.

Sensibly, de Robeck pulled back and licked his wounds. 18 March 1915 is a revered national day of remembrance in Turkey – it was the day their brave gunners sent the British fleet packing.

Some historians argue that had de Robeck returned to the fight immediately he might have ultimately prevailed. Some go further and claim that the Turkish commanders thought the British would return and had given their men orders to fire off their remaining ammunition and withdraw inland.

Whatever the possibilities, the losses of 18 March saw a complete rethink by the British. They adopted Plan B: take the Peninsula with land forces supported by the navy. The strategy's chief proponent was Winston Churchill, who was undeterred by the massive naval setback and now enthusiastically promoted the combined land–sea attack.

Not everyone was as enthusiastic. Britain's First Sea Lord, Lord Fisher, was appalled, and wrote to Churchill:

> 'You are just simply eaten up by the Dardanelles and cannot think of anything else. Damn the Dardanelles! They will be our grave!'

CHAPTER SIX

Ready for a Fight

Although he'd refused to provide troops previously, Lord Kitchener now moved swiftly and created the Mediterranean Expeditionary Force to attack the Dardanelles. He placed a seasoned veteran, 62-year-old General Sir Ian Hamilton, in command. Hamilton had been a soldier for 40 years and had served in Afghanistan, India and the Boer War. He'd twice been recommended for the Victoria Cross and bore the scars of a career of deadly combat: a left hand crippled by a Boer bullet and a bad limp from a riding fall.

Lord Kitchener gave Hamilton a total of 75,000 troops: the 29th British Division (around 18,000); the Anzacs (30,600); a French Division (17,000); and the Royal Naval Division (10,000). But Hamilton had little time to prepare. He was briefed in London and arrived at the Dardanelles just in time to witness the 18 March naval debacle and to begin hurriedly planning for the invasion.

Hamilton wrote in his diary: 'the Peninsula looks a tougher nut to crack than it did on Lord K's small and featureless map.'

The British High Command underestimated the resolve of the Turks who were fighting for their homeland and the lives of their families. It also ignored recent intelligence about the strength and efficiency of the Turkish defences and discounted earlier warnings which estimated at least twice the number of troops proposed would be needed for a successful invasion.

Hamilton simply got on with the job and planned his attack. He knew he'd lost the vital element of surprise. The Turks – through espionage, poor British security (reports had actually appeared in Egyptian papers) and aerial reconnaissance – were well aware an invasion was coming, they just didn't know where.

After the 18 March naval attack, Enver Pasha handed over command of the Ottoman forces at the Dardanelles to a German officer who had been seconded by his government to help reorganise the Ottoman Army before the war. General Otto Liman von Sanders had a massive task ahead of him. He had about 80,000 men to defend 200 kilometres of coastline facing the Aegean Sea as well as the Asian shoreline bordering the Dardanelles. His only chance

AWM G00328

General Sir Ian Hamilton, Commander of the Mediterranean
Expeditionary Force, being rowed ashore at Gallipoli.

was to second-guess Hamilton by anticipating the
locations of the landings.

While von Sanders positioned his defences, the
Allied troops practised their landings on the Greek
island of Lemnos and Hamilton decided on his main
objectives: the forts and the guns on the northern side
of the Narrows. He reasoned that if he could neutralise
them, then the Navy's minesweepers could finally
clear the way at the Narrows so the fleet could enter the
Sea of Marmara and confront Constantinople.

As history has showed, von Sanders guessed well. He anticipated the landings aimed at the forts. His only misjudgement was to commit troops to Bulair, high up in the Gulf of Saros, where he believed Hamilton might move to try to cut off the Peninsula.

The British had already surrendered the greatest advantage of a sea landing – surprise – and they now compounded that loss by breaking a cardinal rule of war: to succeed, an attacking force must have a considerable superiority in numbers to overcome a committed, well-placed defensive force.

AWM J00200

General Otto Liman von Sanders, Commander of the Turkish forces on Gallipoli.

Hamilton had five divisions of about 75,000 troops. Von Sanders had six of around 80,000 troops.

Nonetheless, Hamilton's plan seemed straight-forward: he would land his British and French divisions at the south-west tip of the Gallipoli Peninsula at Cape Helles and the Anzacs about halfway up the western coast, just above the Gaba Tepe headland. The idea was that the British would drive northward and the Anzacs eastward to win the high ground so they could then attack the forts at the Narrows from the rear.

Hamilton decided to split his force into seven sections to confuse the Turks. The French would land on the Asian shore around Kum Kale to hold two of von Sanders' divisions there. The British would land at five small beaches around Cape Helles (codenamed S, V, W, X and Y Beaches). The Anzacs were assigned a longer but equally narrow beach north of Gaba Tepe (Z Beach – later immortalised as Anzac Cove).

Hamilton hoped the Allies would advance towards the Narrows in a classic pincer movement that would simultaneously trap the Turkish defenders and allow the Anzacs to attack the guns at the Narrows' forts, opening the way for the navy to clear the mines there and allow the fleet to proceed on to Constantinople.

Originally, he planned to send the Anzacs across the Maidos Plain to the Narrows, but intelligence received just prior to embarkation showed the Turks had heavily defended this area. Hamilton changed their route to a much more challenging path, up the ravines, gullies and ridgelines that led to Sari Bair (Yellow Ridge) and then on to the Narrows.

The Anzacs' objective for the first day of the landings was to advance the two kilometres or so from their landing point to capture and hold the high point of Sari Bair, code named Hill 971 (it was 971 feet, or about 300 metres, above sea level).

The attacks were planned for 23 April but bad weather forced their postponement for two days.

The Anzacs were champing at the bit.

Charles Bean reported that 100 men sneaked out of their sick beds to join their mates and 100 more tried but were discovered, ruled unfit, and returned to hospital.

The troops were briefed on their roles and objectives in the days prior to the invasion. This was when some of the shortcomings in the plan began to appear: inadequate attention to detail regarding the specifics of the landings and the nature of the terrain that would confront the Anzacs.

From the start, the Anzacs were in an unenviable position: their safest landing place, Anzac Cove, was the worst place to start their charge up the rugged ravines and ridges to Sari Bair; conversely, the best landing spot to assault the heights, Brighton Beach, was the most dangerously exposed to the Turkish artillery.

The Anzacs were divided into two forces: the covering force would land first and secure a toehold and then allow the main force to advance through it on to the high ground.

The 3rd Anzac Brigade (9th, 10th, 11th and 12th Battalions) would be the covering force. They were mainly men from the bush and the mines of Queensland, South and Western Australia and Tasmania. The plan was that the 9th Battalion would be landed to the south and the others would extend across the Anzac position so the 12th was landed at the northern end.

The Victorians' 2nd Brigade would form the main force and the New South Welshmen's 1st Brigade would be the main reserve, available for deployment where needed. Once these had landed, the New Zealand and Australian Division would come ashore.

New Zealand Private Cecil Malthus wrote in his diary:

> 'We have been told that the Australians are to make the first landing, at dawn, and we will reinforce them during the day. We reacted to

this with mixed feelings, in which relief was
the main ingredient ...'

On 24 April 1915 the 200 ships of the massive
invasion armada – battleships, destroyers, transports,
minesweepers, tugs and smaller craft – steamed out of
Mudros Harbour on Lemnos and headed north-east
across a calm Aegean Sea towards the Dardanelles.

Just over halfway to their destination the fleet split:
the ships carrying the Royal Naval Division and some

AWM G00549

Transports anchored in Mudros Harbour, with French soldiers in the
foreground, before the Gallipoli landings.

New Zealanders headed north up the Gulf of Saros to create a feint aimed at tricking von Sanders into thinking the main landings would be near Bulair (where one of New Zealand's favourite sons, then a young lieutenant, Bernard Freyberg, would win the first of his three Distinguished Service Orders (DSO) before winning the VC in France the following year and going on to become the New Zealand Governor General). Those carrying the British and French Divisions sailed to the tiny island of Tenedos in the Northern Aegean Sea to allow the troops to take their invasion stations. Lastly, the Anzacs' ships headed to nearby Imbros where they prepared for their baptism of fire.

CHAPTER SEVEN

I Order You to Die

As they waited on the decks of their destroyers, the Anzacs talked quietly to their mates or wrote letters to their loved-ones.

Lord Kitchener sent a message to Hamilton, wishing him and his men well and concluding:

> '... The task they have to perform will need all the grit Britishers have never failed to show, and I am confident your troops will victoriously clear the way for the Fleet to advance to Constantinople.'

The Anzacs were well kitted out for the battle. In addition to a rifle and bayonet, each man carried 200 rounds of ammunition in pouches on his belt. Slung over his back in two cotton bags were two days' rations – 'bully beef' (boiled beef in tins – originally fed to French soldiers in the Franco–Prussian War – the French *bouilli* for boiled became *bully*), hard biscuits, tea and sugar. Into his backpack he crammed extra water bottles, a waterproof sheet, empty sandbags and whatever personal effects he could fit in. Most carried a shovel-like entrenching tool down their backs under their packs' cross-straps. Because of the cold, they were told to wear their greatcoats. Packs were fastened so they could be easily slipped off if one of the landing boats sank.

Most of the covering force wore British-style caps rather than their slouch hats so as not to be immediately

AWM AO2781

Men of the 1st Divisional Signal Company being towed towards Anzac Cove at 6 am on the day of the landing.

identifiable to the Turks as the inexperienced units from lands downunder that they undoubtedly were.

Around 2 am on the morning of 25 April 1915, the three battleships carrying the covering force hove to off Gaba Tepe. They lowered their landing boats and the 1500 Australians who would make the first assault clambered silently aboard. Each boat carried 30 to 40 troops and four sailors, and was helmed by a young Royal Navy midshipman – most of them still lads even younger than the youthful Anzacs who sat, packed in like sardines, with rifles pointing up between their knees.

By this stage, Turkish observers had reported the vague outlines of what appeared to be ships. The defences were put on alert. Then the moon disappeared below the horizon and the ships' silhouettes faded to black.

By 4 am the first wave of Anzacs was being towed in lines by steam pinnaces. About 50 metres from land they were set free and the sailors rowed them to shore.

Around 4.30 am their boats crunched on to the pebbly beach. Almost immediately, the Turks opened fire from their trenches in the foothills above them. The first man to set foot on Turkish soil was Lieutenant Duncan Chapman, from Brisbane, of the 9th Battalion. He would survive Gallipoli but die a year later at Pozieres in France.

Young Sapper Roy Denning recalls that fateful morning:

> 'While we were waiting for the pinnace to return, a lifeboat was filling on the starboard side when there was a loud splash. In the half light, a soldier had missed his footing, and burdened with his equipment, fell into the water and sank like a stone.'

By the time the remaining troops were climbing out of the boats, the Turkish fire had intensified. Some

AWM J03022

Part of the 4th Battalion and the mules for the 26th (Jacob's) Indian Mountain Battery landing at 8 am.

AWM A03227

Anzacs struggle to find cover at an exposed outpost in Wire Gully at Anzac Cove. Note how they are still wearing British type hats.

young Anzacs were hit but stayed upright, jammed together with their mates in the boats. Others were shot as they leapt from the boats, or slipped on the smooth stones in the shallows. Many drowned before they could release their packs.

Thankfully, most managed to stumble up the beach and throw themselves down under the cover of the natural 'amphitheatre' that confronted them. By this stage, the bodies of the unlucky ones had begun to litter the beach and stain the small shore break with blood.

LISA COTTON

The view the Anazcs would have faced as they looked up at the Turkish positions in the hills near 'the Sphinx' at Anzac Cove.

As New Zealander Private Cecil Malthus later recalled, the young soldiers heard for the first time, 'that sickening soft thud of shell fragments or bullets meeting human flesh.'

From the outset, chaos reigned. The landing place was nothing like the terrain the Anzacs had been briefed to expect. They'd been anticipating low sandy slopes leading off the beach to a long ridgeline; instead, they were faced with steep cliffs, hills and rough scrubby ravines. The terrain before them would originally have been three spurs leading from the ridge down to the beach but, over the centuries, the middle spur had weathered and collapsed, creating the amphitheatre effect and leaving a towering spear of gravel that bore a bizarre resemblance to the Sphinx (and was immediately so named).

The right-hand spur led up to a plateau, soon to be named Plugge's Plateau (pronounced *pluggie's* after Colonel Plugge of the Auckland Battalion who set up his headquarters there). The left-hand spur would soon be named Walker's Ridge and became the New Zealanders' domain.

Sapper Denning watched as he waited to land:

'Salvo after salvo of shrapnel burst with terrific intensity over troops in the crowded boats, riddling some of them with holes so that they quickly sank, leaving a struggling mass in the water. Badly wounded men clung desperately to lesser-wounded mates in an effort to keep their heads above the bloodstained water.

'Fit men bravely fought to save the wounded and drag to shore the dead. Others struggled, half-swimming, half-wading while the fiendish leaden shower continued to cut down both helper and helped.'

Amplified by the hills, the noise of the gunfire was deafening. The leading troops of the first wave, all jumbled together by the confused landing, paused just long enough to drop their packs and fix their bayonets. Then, on their own initiative or led by officers from different units, they charged up the slopes, confronting the first Turks on Ari Burnu, killing or sending the defenders fleeing.

Some small groups of the 3rd Battalion forged ahead up the ridges and reached the first line of hills but they had no support, soon lost cohesion and called for help and more ammunition. They were driven back when Turkish reinforcements arrived.

On the beach, men and their officers tried to link up, get their bearings and identify their objectives, but the confusion increased with every boat that landed and outpoured ever more troops. The Anzacs had been landed around a headland the Turks called Ari Burnu (or Little Bee Cape) instead of the planned Brighton Beach, about a kilometre to the south.

By 9 am, some 8000 troops were ashore, finding cover where they could in dips in the hard ground as they tried to move ahead against the withering Turkish fire, which by now included heavy artillery bombardments as the Turkish gunners found their range.

Far from wavering, as the British High Command

had predicted, the Turkish defenders fought with
determination and valour. Major Mahmut Bey was
one of the Turkish officers waiting in the hills for the
invasion. He recalls:

> '... the enemy approached the shore in
> lifeboats. When they came into range, our
> men opened fire. Here, for years, the colour
> of the sea had always been the same, but
> now it turned red with the blood of our
> enemies.'

The Turks took advantage of their local knowledge
of the terrain and their small initial defensive force
fought to the last. Private Gordon Craig felt their
presence:

> 'The country was so rough and scrubby that
> you couldn't see where you were going and
> the shrapnel was bursting all round and the
> bullets were so thick that we thought they
> were bees buzzing about us.'

Another Anzac, Albert Facey, then a 20-year-old
Private, was in the second wave of the landings. He
wrote in his autobiography, *A Fortunate Life*:

AWM C02679

Evacuation of wounded from Anzac Cove on barges. Those able to stand or sit were transported on the steam launch *Keraunos*.

'The Turks had machine guns sweeping the strip of beach where we landed ... there were many dead already when we got there. Bodies of men who had reached the beach ahead of us were lying all along the beach and wounded men were screaming for help ... we used our trenching tools to dig mounds of earth and sheltered from the firing until daylight ... the Turks never let up ... the slaughter was terrible.'

Sergeant Baker later wrote home:

> 'Their fire was getting absolutely murderous,
> but our chaps advanced again and again and
> were dropping in all directions, but would not
> be stopped. That Sunday [25 April] should
> live in history, for the Australians proved
> what stuff they were made of and many a one
> made a hero of himself. And many a poor
> fellow died urging his mates onward with his
> last breath. Here is a tragic happening … a
> chap that had half his face blown off was seen
> to coolly finish himself off with his own rifle.
> One of his mates was with him at the time.'

Despite the ferocity of the Australian assault, the
Turks held firm. Their determination to fight for their
homeland was exemplified by the order given by the
officer in charge of the Turkish reserve division at
Bigali (inland from Anzac Cove), Lieutenant Colonel
Mustafa Kemal:

> 'I don't order you to attack, I order you to die.
> In the time it takes us to die, other troops and
> commanders can come and take our place.'

Shortly after the landing, a salvo of British naval shells crashed on to the top of the first ridge above the beachhead. It woke Kemal. Unable to reach his commander, General von Sanders, who had gone to Bulair where he expected the main landing force, Kemal used his own initiative and gambled. It was a decision that would change the outcome of the entire campaign.

Rather than direct his troops to the Allies' landing area at Anzac Cove, Kemal sent them straight to the high ground, about 3 kilometres inland from it – the spot he knew was the key to holding the Peninsula.

Ironically, when Kemal gave this order, the Turks and the Anzacs were equidistant from this key ground, but because the Anzacs had been landed at Anzac Cove and not at Brighton Beach, they found themselves bush-bashing their way up the steep gullies above Plugge's Plateau through a relentless hail of bullets.

Kemal's 57th Battalion had a much easier route and he led the way and rushed a considerable distance ahead of his men to observe the landings. He was in front of the defensive lines at the high ground near a point later called Baby 700 when a group of the first Turkish defenders fled past him in full retreat, crying that they were out of ammunition.

Just then the first Anzacs appeared.

AWM A05318

Ataturk, observing the action at Gallipoli.

AWM G00410

A view from the heights above Anzac Cove looking north towards
Suvla Bay, showing the broken ground over which the Anzacs later
advanced during the battle of Sari Bair.

Kemal was caught between the invaders and his
own lines. He ordered the wavering Turks to fix their
bayonets, form a line and take cover.

When the Anzacs saw the Turks taking cover,
they followed suit. Immediately, Kemal seized the
opportunity – he rushed back and ordered his men
into their defensive positions on the high ground.
They made it just ten minutes ahead of the Anzacs.

Turkish historians believe that this ten minutes changed the course of the campaign. Many argue that this ten minutes changed history.

Had the Anzacs reached the dominating heights at Chunuk Bair in sufficient numbers, it's unlikely the Turks could have held the Peninsula. Once the

The view the Turks would have had of the Anzac Cove landing area from the high ground above the beaches.

Allies had secured the Narrows they would have taken Constantinople; they could then have resupplied the faltering Russian Army, and this may have avoided the collapse in 1916 that opened the way for the communist revolution the following year. Russia may have conquered Turkey (as was the secret Allied plan), the Tsar may have had sufficient power to stave off the communists and Ataturk would have never have risen to power ...

All this, but for that critical ten minutes.

In the early stages of the fighting, as skirmishes raged through the ravines and up and down the hills, there was considerable fluidity and movement. Positions were won and lost a number of times and both sides were unsure of their front lines. But gradually the Turkish reinforcements held up the Anzacs' advance and the front lines became defined.

By 4 pm all the assault troops were ashore. As night fell the Anzacs had established their beachhead around Anzac Cove. It extended along the shore for about a kilometre and in a wedge pointing inland for a similar distance – in total an area of about 160 hectares within a perimeter of about two kilometres.

Although the beachhead was won, it came at a terrible cost. About 2000 Anzac troops were killed and at least 1700 wounded on that one day.

Captain John Whitham of the AIF's 12th Battalion was full of admiration for those Anzacs who were wounded:

> 'Badly wounded, horribly wounded, men would stick it all with hardly a murmur. And there was not much in the way of attention for them for the first 24 hours. The stretcher bearers and the ambulance men were just splendid, but their work was heavy and they had many casualties themselves.'

The Anzacs' commander, General Birdwood, thought the landing was a disaster and doubted his men could withstand another day like it. He wrote to his Commander in Chief, Sir Ian Hamilton, seeking permission to evacuate:

> '... if troops are subjected to shell fire tomorrow morning [26 April] there is likely to be a fiasco as I have no fresh troops with which to replace those in the firing line. I know my representation is most serious but if we are to re-embark it must be at once.'

Hamilton replied at 2.30 am on 26 April:

'Your news is indeed serious. But there is
nothing for it but to dig yourselves right in
and stick it out. It would take at least two days
to re-embark.'

Charles Bean had landed with the second wave and later
wrote that he believed the Anzacs expected the Turks
to counter-attack at first light and were determined to
fight to the last man to hold the beach.

But the counter-attack didn't come straightaway
and the Anzacs took advantage of the lull to strengthen
their defences while landing even more of their
troops.

Later that morning the Turks finally counter-
attacked in great numbers but the Anzacs fought back
fiercely and held their lines. The battle raged during
the day as both sides poured in reinforcements and by
nightfall the Anzacs had held on.

Captain Whitham recalls:

'The behaviour of the lads was just splendid,
even when their leaders were gone they kept
well to the front, and despite their losses,
never lost heart. There were times when
portions of the line had to fall back, having
gone, perhaps, too far forward, or having met

with close range fire from concealed rifles
and machine guns, but they were always ready
to rally.'

The next day, 27 April, the Turks again threw themselves
against the Anzacs' trenches and bombarded the beach
to try to stop supplies and reinforcements landing.
The British battleships countered by bombarding the
Turkish gun emplacements in the high ground.

Still the Anzacs hung on.

They were developing a grudging respect for their
enemy, as Lieutenant Richard Thomas Tarrant of the
2nd Battalion, later wrote in a letter to his mother:

'On Tuesday morning the 27th (Harry's
birthday) at 6 am, I was sent out on a patrol to
look for "snipers". Those are men who must
be looked upon as having grit, even though
they are Turks. They creep up by themselves,
as close as they can, and "pot" anybody off
that comes within sight. They nearly always
lose their lives as they are sure to get caught.'

The Anzacs were tough as well. One soldier reported
to the regimental aid post saying he'd been wounded
at the landing and had fought on but was now having

'a little trouble'. The medical officer found that the soldier had a compound fracture of the arm, two bullets through his thigh and another through the diaphragm, liver and side. Not surprisingly, the doctor confined him to bed and later shipped him home. But after he recuperated in Australia, he re-enlisted and returned to fight in Europe in the artillery!

Over the ensuing days, while the Australians and New Zealanders consolidated their beachhead, elsewhere the fighting degenerated into the very trench warfare the campaign had been designed to avoid.

AWM H03500

The confusion of troops and stores on the beach at Anzac Cove, showing boats in the background and some men bathing.

The Anzacs dug their trenches and shelters deeper and Anzac Cove expanded into a mini port with jetties, floating bridges and pontoons servicing an endless stream of boats and lighters bringing stores ashore.

The beach was now crammed with mountains of food, water, ammunition and equipment; rough shelters, a wireless station, ambulances, dressing stations, mountain guns and mules. It looked more like some misplaced wild-west shantytown than the deadly battlefield it was.

CHAPTER EIGHT

Gallipoli Stalemate

While the Anzacs fought for their lives, General Hamilton watched anxiously from his flagship as he received confused reports from the other landings.

From the start, the operation was hamstrung by several factors that combined to diminish its effectiveness and, ultimately, doom it to failure. The split command structure was inefficient at best and counter-productive at worst. Communications were unreliable; the navy's bombardment was inaccurate; and many of Hamilton's subordinate commanders were simply not up to the task.

In the tradition of the British Army at the time, Hamilton handed executive command to Major General Aylmer Hunter-Weston (known to the troops as Hunter-Bunter), Commanding Officer of the British 29th Division, while Hamilton and his staff waited offshore. To add to the communications problems, Hunter-Weston also established his command centre onboard a ship.

The men of the 29th Division landed at S, V, W, X and Y Beaches around the heel of Cape Helles and Krithia, starting about half an hour after the Anzacs first wave had hit the shore.

They met with mixed receptions. Those who landed at Y Beach, adjacent to Krithia, were unopposed and S and X Beaches were secured with minimal casualties.

That was the good news.

From then on, everything went bad. At W Beach, the Lancashire Fusiliers faced barbed-wire entanglements and unyielding defenders who savaged them with machine-gun fire as they landed. In the chaotic fighting that ensued, the Lancashires won their now famous 'six VCs before breakfast' but suffered devastating losses – 533 casualties out of 950 in less than an hour.

Nevertheless, they did manage to establish a beachhead and, supported by some accurate naval gunnery, forced the Turks back.

The losses at V Beach, near the old fort at Seddulbahir, were just as bad. An old collier, *The River Clyde*, had been converted as a landing craft and carried 2000 men from the Munster and Hampshire Regiments. It landed at V Beach and unloaded its troops into a hailstorm of lead from the well-entrenched and well-armed defenders. The Allies were caught in the open and had little chance of survival.

Hunter-Weston watched the events unfold from his ship off Cape Helles. Reports were confused and contradictory and he apparently did not know or understand the opportunity that Y Beach offered to push inland to the high ground. Rather than land his reserves there unopposed, he poured them into the bloodbath at V Beach. When Hamilton eventually heard of the situation at Y Beach, he offered trawlers to Hunter-Weston to land reserves there but was rebuffed.

British Brigadier-General CF Aspinall-Oglander later wrote:

> 'It is as certain as anything can be in war that a bold advance from Y on morning of the twenty-fifth of April must have freed the southern beaches that morning and ensured a decisive victory for the 29th Division.'

Any chance of success at Cape Helles was squandered. Despite their massive losses, the British outnumbered the defenders but their inability to break out of V Beach, where *The River Clyde* initiative turned to disaster, saw the landings degenerate into yet another stalemate.

With the benefit of hindsight (and considerable analysis), we now know that 25 April 1915 held the greatest chance for success for the invasion. The Allies temporarily had the numbers. Had they been able to coordinate their forces and rush inland to overwhelm the confused Turkish garrison troops, they may have won a relatively cheap victory.

By the next day, the position had changed considerably. As the Turkish reinforcements surged in, any chances of an Allied victory quickly evaporated.

At Anzac Cove, as the days ground on, the campaign degenerated further into static trench warfare with its constant sniping, grenade throwing, tunnelling and patrolling, all carried out beneath the persistent artillery bombardment. The fighting took an ever-growing toll on both sides.

The impact of the Anzac casualties can be seen from the fate of the 16th Battalion AIF. By early May, Signaller Ellis Silas was one of the few of the 16th left to answer the roll call. He recalls:

> '… how heartbreaking it is – name after name is called; the reply a deep silence which can be felt, despite the noise of the incessant cracking of rifles and screaming of shrapnel …'

In fact, of the 16th's 1207 men who had landed on 25 April 1915, just 450 were able to answer when their names were called some two weeks later — 757 had been either killed or wounded or were missing.

The toll grew on 5 and 6 May, when the New Zealand Infantry Brigade and the Australian 2nd Brigade were shipped south to the British front at Cape Helles. There, over the following three days, together with French and other colonial troops, the Allies attacked the Turks at Krithia, the ancient stone town that had earlier been levelled by British naval bombardment.

The beach at Anzac Cove on 26 August 1915, showing the hillside as yet uninhabited.

Advancing across two kilometres of open country into the teeth of the Turkish guns, the Allies were cut down and beaten off. The Anzacs barely made it halfway, losing 1000 men – a third of their number – in the process.

Towards the end of May, a degree of Anzac ingenuity came to fruition. Sydneysider Lance Corporal William Beech, of the 2nd Battalion AIF, invented a 'periscope rifle' that allowed soldiers to fire from their trenches without exposing themselves. Anzac engineers quickly capitalised on the invention and started a factory at Anzac Cove making the rifles using mirrors scrounged from the support ships. The invention would save many Anzac lives and inflict countless casualties on the Turks.

Throughout the campaign, the Anzacs existed on a monotonous and inadequate diet. In the first months, each man was responsible for cooking for himself. Breakfast was black tea and sugar, dog biscuits (six a day), jam and a small piece of cheese and one rasher of bacon; lunch was just tea, usually no food; while dinner was bully beef or stew and tea.

As soon as the intensity of the fighting eased, disease took hold. The unsanitary environment bred incessant flies and lice which led to endless bouts of dysentery, enteric fever and diarrhoea.

AWM HO2310

An Anzac using a periscope rifle, invented by Lance Corporal (later Sergeant) WCB Beech of the 2nd Battalion.

The lice caused particular discomfort and sorely tested morale. Soldiers fell into a daily routine of 'chatting' – sitting with their clothing on their knees crushing the lice in the seams. Lieutenant Frank Boyes of the 12th Battalion AIF reckoned the lice were worse than the Turks:

AWM C01828

Four unidentified soldiers enjoy the sunshine while 'chatting' (delousing) their clothing near Bloody Angle between Pope's Hill and Quinn's Post on the Gallipoli Peninsula.

'They lived and bred mainly in the seams of the inner garments and as there was no hot water or chemicals available for their control or destruction the field was open for them to multiply and flourish ... We veterans of the 1st War were unanimous in declaring that the "chats" on Gallipoli were harder to endure than all the Turks, tucker and all the other conditions combined.'

The experience lives on today in words, handed down by the soldiers: 'lousy' – lice-infested, and 'crummy' – because the lice looked like bread crumbs.

Morale continued to decline under the strain of constant combat, the enervating heat, the poor food, the lack of water, the vermin and the subsequent sickness. At Anzac Cove, the troops were under constant shellfire of one kind or another. They also had to contend with poor nutrition, problems with their water supply, inadequate medicines and no proper dental treatment.

There were no canteen or Red Cross stores and mail was sporadic, fortnightly at best. There was nowhere the men could go to seek relief from the tension of combat. As one Anzac ruefully said: 'Of all the bastards of places this is the greatest bastard in the world.'

The situation continued to deteriorate and by the end of July, the Anzacs on Gallipoli were losing around 200 men a day to sickness. Most were being repatriated to Cairo in Egypt.

As summer approached the number of flies increased and descended on the killing fields. They fed on the dead and contaminated the Anzacs' food. Cecil Malthus recalls:

'Dozens of flies were drowned in every dixie of tea we drank and they would chase the food into our very mouths. The dust in the bottom of the trenches, in which we slept, was alive with maggots.'

The soldiers' only relief was a brief swim in the sea and men regularly braved the ever-present Turkish artillery or occasional snipers for this smallest of pleasures. They would soak their clothes to kill the lice even though they knew there were countless more that would take their place as soon as they returned to their trenches.

Cecil Malthus adds:

'A trip to the beach was faintly reminiscent of a visit to town in happier days. The beach was the centre of life at Anzac [Cove]. There one could bathe and wash clothes in the sea, admire the incredible physique of some truly god-like Australians, pick up the latest gossip and even buy special provisions, at special rates, from the sailors who came ashore.'

CHAPTER NINE

A Time for Heroes

On 19 May 1915, the Anzacs were on full alert, having learned of a Turkish counter-attack in the pre-dawn hours.

The Turkish Commander, General von Sanders, had gathered four divisions – around 42,000 troops, more than twice the number of Anzacs – in the valleys behind the front lines. Luckily, British naval reconnaissance planes had detected them and warned the Australians and New Zealanders.

The attack came around 3 am when the Turks charged across a wide front. The Anzacs held their nerve and inflicted heavy casualties – almost 10,000 Turks were downed in the first two hours alone – for the loss of 160 killed and 468 wounded. The Allies rebuffed the Turks all along the front, except at Courtney's Post, next to Quinn's Post, where the ground favoured the attackers. There the Turks overran part of the Anzac trench system and looked certain to break through their perimeter.

AWM C01541

Anzac sniper uses his periscope rifle while his mate observes for him.

Troops of the 14th Battalion managed to block the Turks' progress to the south, but only a lone soldier, Lance Corporal Albert Jacka, stood in their way to the north.

Lieutenant Crabbe asked Jacka if he could retake the position. Jacka replied that with support he could charge the Turks.

Soon after, Jacka and three volunteers charged out of their trench. Almost immediately the other two were hit and fell. Jacka saw their path was blocked. He regrouped and arranged that Crabbe and the others

AWM P02141

Corporal Albert Jacka VC, outside his tent. Jacka won the first VC awarded to the AIF for his gallantry at Courtney's Post.

stage a diversion while he sneaked behind the Turks. Distracted by grenades and the covering fire, the Turks were stunned when Jacka materialised out of the smoke, leaping over the parapet into their trench. He shot five and bayoneted two. The others fled. Jacka picked off two more as they ran.

When Lieutenant Crabbe and the others reached the position, Jacka was sitting calmly amid the bodies, an unlit cigarette in his mouth.

'I managed to get the beggars, sir,' was his greeting.

For his remarkable single-handed efforts, Albert Jacka was awarded the first of the nine Australian Victoria Crosses to be won in the Gallipoli campaign.

The Victoria Cross, or VC as it is commonly known, is the highest award for bravery for British and Commonwealth armed forces. It can only be awarded for 'most conspicuous bravery, or some daring or pre-eminent act of valour or self-sacrifice or extreme devotion to duty in the presence of the enemy'. Only 1355 VCs have been awarded since its creation during the Crimean War in 1854. A total of 626 VCs were awarded in World War I, 66 to Australians, 18 to New Zealanders.

Another event of 19 May 1915 has entered Australian folklore: the gallant Private John Simpson was killed by machine-gun fire in Monash Gully as he attempted to rescue another fallen mate.

Simpson had landed at Anzac Cove at 5 am on 25 April as part of the 3rd Field Ambulance of the 1st Australian Division AIF. For 24 days, from 26 April, he carried on a self-appointed role rescuing wounded Anzacs and carrying them back to the beach aid post on a donkey he'd scrounged.

He worked up and down the perilous ravines with complete disregard for the snipers and shrapnel that swept across the positions. Every day the troops

AWM J06392

The legendary John Simpson Kirkpatrick (known as Simpson on Gallipoli) carrying another wounded man to safety on his donkey.

would watch in awe from their dugouts as Simpson crawled through the scrub then dashed out to recover a wounded man trapped in the open. Often they burst into applause as he hauled his patient back and put him on his donkey that waited patiently under cover.

Simpson would start work around 6.30 am in the morning and often was still out there at 3 am the following. He quickly became a living legend among his fellow soldiers.

He was born John Simpson Kirkpatrick in England and grew up in South Shields before becoming a merchant seaman at the age of 17. He first worked in the Mediterranean but on a trip to Newcastle (in Australia) in 1910 he jumped ship and travelled to his newly-adopted country working as a cane cutter and a gold and coal miner before returning to the sea on coastal ships.

When war was declared he jumped ship again in Perth in August 1914 and enlisted, probably hoping for a free trip back to the UK. Fearing rejection as a merchant marine deserter, he dropped his surname when he enlisted and became known to his Anzac mates as 'Simmie, the man with the donkey'.

He was revered by all, not only because of his extraordinary bravery and devotion to the wounded, but also because of his constant good humour and his larrikin approach to authority.

Padre Green spoke at his burial service at Beach Cemetery:

> 'If ever there was a man who deserved the Victoria Cross it was Simpson. I often remember now the scene I saw frequently in Shrapnel Gully of that cheerful soul calmly walking down the gully with a Red Cross armlet tied round the donkey's head.'

Despite his remarkable achievements, and although he was twice recommended for the VC, Simpson received no medal. Today, he lies in the Beach Cemetery at Anzac Cove. His gravestone bears the simple inscription: 'He gave his life that others may live.' He was just 22 when he died.

The day after the bloody 19 May attacks, unofficial truces broke out along the front line as each side recovered the dead and wounded from no-man's land. On 24 May, the gruesome task was completed under a formal armistice.

For the first time the two sides saw each other face to face. They exchanged tokens of photos and cigarettes. One Anzac who helped with the burials later told Roy Denning:

Turkish and Anzac soldiers recover and bury the bodies of dead comrades killed during the Turks' attack on Anzac positions.

'The dead of both sides were horribly mixed as we tried to sort them out for a decent burial. The old bloke [a Turkish soldier] was near me when he pulled out a packet of cigarettes and lit one, and before I realised what I was doing, I was beside him and lighting my fag off his match. Then a funny feeling came over me. This is the enemy; in a couple of short hours I'll be doing my best to kill this old bugger and he'll be doing his best to kill me.'

On this day, the seeds of respect were sown. The Anzacs began calling their enemy 'Johnny Turk', 'Jacko' and 'Abdul' – with typical grudging Australian respect for an honourable foe — and from then on the Anzacs were keenly aware they were fighting men who were, like them, just doing their best for their country.

One of the most dangerous positions at Anzac Cove was Quinn's Post, the most advanced spot on the Anzac front line and the furthest from the sea. It was the key

AWM G01005

Russell's Top, Pope's Hill and Quinn's Post.

to the entire Anzac position – in military terms 'the ground of tactical importance', the ground without which your position is untenable. Charles Bean said he watched men in Monash Gully staring up at the fighting at Quinn's Post 'as they might at a haunted house'. Had the Turks been able to capture Quinn's they would have been able to exert almost irresistible pressure on the Anzac position.

To reach Quinn's Post you had to wind your way through a series of deep communication trenches, then up Shrapnel Gully and Monash Gully, before mounting a long straight staircase made from faggots of

AWM G01026

Anzac shelters at Quinn's Post, looking towards Pope's and Russell's Top.

brushwood. If you looked up the head of Monash Gully you'd see Pope's Hill dominating the deep ravines on either side of it. High on the right-hand side, clinging to the side of the steep cliff, was Quinn's Post. Further back to the right on the cliffside was Courtney's Post.

Quinn's Post was in fact a series of six mini-posts, each containing about 20 men. Some of these were almost within touching distance of the opposing Turkish trenches.

One Digger who served at Quinn's Post said, 'the ground itself seemed to be wounded and bleeding.'

After visiting Quinn's Post later in the campaign, Sir Ian Hamilton wrote in his diary:

> 'Men live through more in five minutes on
> that crest than they do in five years in Bendigo
> or Ballarat.'

The position was named after Major Hugh Quinn of Townsville from the 15th Battalion who commanded it in the early fighting. He was killed on 29 May 1915 as his men regained the position after the Turks had exploded a mine under one of the Anzac trenches.

Later, the New Zealanders took over at Quinn's Post and held on heroically as they endured relentless Turkish grenade throwing and sniper attacks. The

Turks took full advantage of their superior position and looking over the parapet was tantamount to suicide. The tension at Quinn's Post eventually took its toll on all its inhabitants, as Cecil Malthus wrote:

> 'If hitherto I had any zeal for the business, the sickening terror of those tense watches dispelled it. To lie cowering in the darkness of that cramped and evil-smelling pit, and watch a big bomb sputtering among the corpses just against our loophole, while waiting for the burst, was an experience no man could endure unmoved.'

CHAPTER TEN

The Heat of August

One of the most remarkable events of the Gallipoli Campaign was the fighting that took place at Lone Pine during what became known as the 'August Offensive'.

General Hamilton knew that in order to have any sort of success, he had to find some way of breaking out of the narrow beachheads. Lord Kitchener had sent Hamilton five more British divisions to be used on the Peninsula to break the deadlock. Hamilton planned to land them behind the salt lake at Suvla Bay, about 8 kilometres north of Anzac Cove, so they could attack the high ground.

But when they landed, in a classic example of 'he who hesitates is lost', their commander wasted three days waiting offshore aboard the yacht, *Jonquil*, for heavier artillery pieces to be sent from Egypt.

The 61-year-old Lieutenant General Sir Frederick Stopford had recently come out of retirement and had never led troops in combat. Had he acted immediately, he may have turned the tide. When his force landed, just 1500 Turkish defenders stood against his 70,000 fresh British soldiers.

The Turkish Commander, General von Sanders, did not hesitate. He rushed his two divisions from the Isthmus to confront the British.

Some of the bloodiest fighting of the entire campaign was about to erupt.

For months Hamilton and his command had worked on a plan to move men and equipment to the left flank of the Anzac position to stage a major assault aimed at capturing the vital high ground at Chunuk Bair. Over the weeks, the British 13th Division, the New Zealand troops, a division of Australians and a brigade of Gurkhas had quietly moved into position on the left without raising Turkish suspicions.

An integrated plan was conceived involving a number of diversions to cover the main thrust on the left and at Suvla. One of these involved the Australians at Lone Pine.

On the very first day of the Anzac landings, some Victorians from the 6th Battalion had made it up to Lone Pine on the extreme right of the Anzac position but they lacked support and were forced back by Turkish reinforcements. It remained a key objective from then on.

Lone Pine is a flat, exposed ridge top with views to the Aegean Sea and the island of Imbros on the horizon. It is named for its only feature, a single Aleppo Pine tree. The Anzacs originally named it 'Lonesome Pine' after an American song, 'On the Trail of the Lonesome Pine', which was popular around the start of the war.

The lone pine which thrives on the site today is a descendant of the original tree which was destroyed during the fighting. After the Allies captured the position, a sergeant who lost a brother there picked

LISA COTTON

Lone Pine Memorial today. The Anzac positions were near the gravestones in the foreground, the Turkish trenches were under the stone monolith under which soldiers from both sides now lie intermingled.

up a cone from one of the dead tree's branches and sent it home to his mother as a keepsake. She raised a tree from seeds shed by the cone and later presented that tree to the Australian War Memorial in Canberra where it still lives, south-west of the main building. Seedlings from this tree have subsequently spread around Australia and one was returned to the battlesite at Lone Pine.

Although it was designed as a distraction, in the end the assault on Lone Pine resulted in some of the bloodiest hand-to-hand fighting of the entire campaign.

AWM A00847

Anzacs moving up to go into the line on the southern part of Lone Pine.

During four days of conflict in an area the size of two tennis courts, more than 4000 Turkish soldiers and 2200 Anzacs fought and died for their countries. This battle also yielded an unprecedented seven Victoria Crosses.

Lone Pine was warfare at its most primitive – gladiatorial combat to the death. Men fought with bullets, bayonets, rifle butts, fists, even boots, literally standing on the corpses of their mates and their enemy.

The Turks had a more appropriate name for Lone Pine: they called it *Kanlisirt* or Bloody Ridge.

During the battle, several rows of Turkish trenches were directly beneath where the main Australian memorial stands today. The Australian trenches were in six rows under where the gravestones now lie. Just a couple of cricket pitches separated the two front lines.

Charles Bean reported a classic example of mateship as the Anzacs counted down the final minutes before the assault:

> 'By 5 o'clock the 1st Brigade was in position, crowding below the openings in the underground line and on the firestep of the old, deep, open trenches 50 yards behind.

"Can you find room for me beside Jim here?" said an Australian who had been searching along the bays. "Him and me are mates an' we're going over together."'

The Anzacs had sewn white armbands and white patches on their backs so they could recognise one another in the silver moonlight. Australians from the 1st, 2nd, 3rd and 4th (New South Wales) Battalions; 7th (Victorian) Battalion and 12th Battalion (South Australians and Tasmanians) — all original Anzacs — rose from their trenches and surged towards the Turks at around 5.30 pm on 6 August under a full moon.

They found Turkish trenches heavily fortified with overhead log cover. While some tried to break through the logs under terrible fire, others charged around the side and attacked along the communication trenches. In murderous close-combat fighting the Anzacs eventually prevailed and before nightfall they claimed the enemy position.

Realising the significance of the position, the Turks counter-attacked with reinforcements during the night, raining down grenades on the advancing Allies. Turkish grenades resembled cast-iron cricket balls with an external fuse of a few seconds' duration that they lit before throwing. They were notoriously unpredictable.

Anzacs inside a captured Turkish trench at Lone Pine.

AWM P02939.007

Portrait of Lieutenant (Lt) Leonard Keysor VC, 1st Battalion.

Lance Corporal Len Keysor, a London-born member of the 1st Battalion, staged an astounding performance of bravery and endurance in dealing with the grenades. As the Turks lobbed their bombs (as the soldiers called them) into the Australian trenches, Keysor would leap forward and smother the explosions with sandbags, occasionally even with his greatcoat. Sometimes, if the fuse allowed him the time, he would catch the bomb in mid-flight or snatch it up and return it to the sender with deadly effect. Although wounded, Len Keysor kept up his 'fielding' continuously for 50 hours before he consented to being evacuated for treatment. He won the first VC at Lone Pine.

At the end of the four-day battle, for the first and only time since the landings, the Turks withdrew. But they set up a new trench line just 39 metres behind their previous positions. For the sake of two tennis courts' worth of land, more than 6000 soldiers perished. In one battalion alone, of the 27 officers and 576 men who began the attack, 21 officers and 420 men died.

As the Turks retreated, one Anzac wag yelled from his trench: 'Play ya again next Saturday!'

The Anzacs were awarded nine VCs over an eight-month period at Gallipoli – seven of them in three days at Lone Pine. In addition to Len Keysor, Lieutenant William Symons, Corporal Alexander Burton, Corporal William Dunstan, Private John Hamilton, Lieutenant Frederick Tubb and Captain Alfred Shout all won the highest award for valour.

Even the Turks were impressed, as one captured sergeant said:

> 'We will go out to meet the French, we will wait for the British to come up to our trenches, but the Australians we will not face and no amount of driving will make us do so.'

AWM C01685

Looking back from Lone Pine to the jumping off trench from which the 1st Australian Infantry Brigade commenced its successful Anzac attack.

Lieutenant Roy Harrison later wrote to his cousin, Emily:

> 'The place was choked with dead and wounded, and in many places, it was impossible to avoid walking over the dead.
>
> 'When light came, the second morning after the assault, the trenches were three deep with dead and wounded and, in one particular trench, were four deep. To pass along, it was necessary to crawl over the dead and the living ... The sights and sounds come up to anything I have yet read, and surpassing my wildest dreams as to what war really meant.'

Today, the Lone Pine Memorial is the principal Australian memorial on the Gallipoli Peninsula. It is sacred to both sides and is the largest mass grave on Gallipoli. Australian and Turkish soldiers are here forever linked in death's embrace. The memorial also marks the farthest point of the Australian advance – a paltry 1.2 kilometres from the beachhead at Anzac Cove.

The intensity of the fighting at Lone Pine can be seen in exhibits in the war museum at Gabatepe, a couple of kilometres to the south. There, a glass cabinet displays a dozen or so 'fused' bullets – bullets (from opposing rifles) which have not only collided mid-flight but have become embedded in each other.

Around the same time as Lone Pine, as part of the August Offensive, Hamilton ordered the Anzacs to mount another heroic, but ultimately pointless, assault on an exposed ridgeline called The Nek. This doomed attack against entrenched Turkish machine guns was the centrepiece of Peter Weir's evocative movie, *Gallipoli*.

Like Lone Pine, the charge at The Nek was aimed at diverting Turkish reserves from the main push on the left and at Suvla Bay. The Nek assault was to be by the famous 3rd Australian Light Horse Brigade, minus their mounts which had been left in Egypt.

The Nek is a narrow saddle of land which runs east–west along the ridgeline between two hills – Russell's Top and Baby 700 – before dropping away sharply on both sides into a valley 150 metres below. The Turks waited in eight lines of well-protected trenches rising with the hill line to the top of Baby 700. All were covered by nests of machine guns that could fire on any movement below. Many believe it was the strongest Turkish position on the Peninsula.

By the time the Light Horse Brigade was in position for the attack, the supporting actions elsewhere,

A bullet found by the author in the carpark of the Lone Pine Memorial in 2002.

The Memorial at The Nek, scene of the action featured in Peter Weir's movie *Gallipoli*.

which may have given them some glimmer of success, had either failed or faltered. Their only hope was a planned artillery barrage which should have battered the Turkish defenders and kept their machine gunners under cover.

The bombardment was scheduled to run for half an hour, starting at 4 am and ending with three minutes of intense shelling. The Australians were set to charge in four lines of 150 men (the most they could fit) at exactly 4.30 am. But, either because of poor synchronisation of watches or a misunderstanding, the shelling suddenly stopped at 4.23 am – seven minutes early. Unsure whether it would resume, the Anzacs held to the original timetable. The Turks had time to emerge from cover and man their weapons and when the Anzacs charged, they ran into a lethal hail of lead.

Charles Bean reported:

'The Australian line, now charging, was seen suddenly to go limp, and then sink to the earth, as though [said an eye-witness] "the men's limbs had become string". Except those wounded whom bullets had knocked back into the trench, or who managed to crawl a few yards and drop into it. Almost the

whole line fell dead or dying within the first
ten yards.'

Despite witnessing the carnage, the second line of
Anzacs jumped up without hesitation when their turn
came. They barely made it past the first line of corpses.
Amid reports that some of the troops had made it close
to the Turkish lines, the attack continued. The third
line answered the whistle and was cut down.

The fourth and final line was held for an agonising
half hour as their leaders sought confirmation to
continue before a tragic misunderstanding saw an
officer, who was unaware of the reasons for the delay,
call for the final charge. The right side of the last line
leapt into action and drew the rest with them.

Dawn broke on what remained of the pride of the
Light Horse Brigade, strewn in front of the Australian
trenches in an area no bigger than a tennis court.

Charles Bean recorded:

> 'At first here and there a man raised his arm
> to the sky, or tried to drink from his water
> bottle. But as the sun of that burning day
> climbed higher, such movement ceased. Over
> the whole summit the figures lay still in the
> quivering heat.'

AWM G00599

Mateship in action: an Anzac carries a wounded comrade to safety.
North Beach and Sulva Bay are in the background.

Of the 600 Light Horsemen who charged at The Nek, more than half were injured and 234 of them were killed.

As Bean wrote: 'The flower of the youth of Victoria and Western Australia fell in that attempt'.

The Turks had another name for The Nek. They called it *Cesarit Tepe* (or Hill of Valour).

CHAPTER ELEVEN

Kiwi Glory

The New Zealanders played a leading role in the August Offensive, achieving dramatic gains during the breakout.

On the left flank, alongside the British troops, the Wellington Battalion fought heroically in the gullies and ridges leading to the high ground. Charles Bean called their actions 'a magnificent feat of arms, the brilliance of which was never surpassed if indeed equalled during the campaign.'

The New Zealand Mounted Rifles (on foot) attacked up the gullies leading to Sari Bair along Chunuk Bair and Hill 971. They took advantage of the Turks' habit of taking cover each evening before the regular naval bombardment. The Auckland Mounteds rushed the Turkish position and took it without losing a single man.

The New Zealand Infantry Brigade, along with the Sikhs and Gurkhas and the 4th Australian Infantry Brigade, followed up and seized Chunuk Bair. Cecil Malthus recalls the moment with justifiable pride:

AWM G01287

A deserted Anzac Cove during the final days of the evacuation.

'So, for the first time since the landing there
were Anzac troops on the summit of Sari Bair
gazing down on the Narrows, just a glimpse of
a path of water to the south-east.'

Nearby, a small band of Gurkhas took control of
another summit known as Q but were outnumbered
and driven back.

There were many heroes among the New
Zealanders, and although several were recommended
for the VC, only one was awarded. On Chunuk Bair,

under relentless fire, Corporal Cyril Bassett, a tiny New Zealand signaller, exemplified his countrymen's unbreakable courage when he kept his unit's communications alive by constantly crawling and dashing out under fire in full daylight to repair his telephone wire. His award was not for a number of brave actions, but like his mates, for sustained valour over days.

Bassett fell ill shortly afterwards and was evacuated. He was stunned to learn while he recuperated that he'd been awarded the VC. Years later he said:

> 'When I got the medal I was disappointed to find I was the only New Zealander to get one at Gallipoli, because hundreds of Victoria Crosses should have been awarded there. All my mates ever got were wooden crosses.'

By 9 August, the New Zealanders were hanging on, but under intolerable pressure, as Cecil Malthus noted:

> 'Bombed, shelled, sniped, raked with machine-gun fire, suffering extremely from thirst, they utterly refused to be dislodged, but they could only get some relief from time to time by getting out and charging with the

bayonet or catching the Turkish bombs and hurling them back. And all day the sun blazed down on their agony. This was perhaps New Zealand's finest hour.'

In the hours before dawn on 10 August, the New Zealand forward troops were relieved by British units from North Lancashire and Wiltshire. But they had barely had time to settle in, and hadn't even seen their new position in daylight, before the Turks, led by Mustafa Kemal, counter-attacked in great numbers.

They swept the British troops from the hill but were held up by a savage rear-guard action by New Zealand machine-gunners. Caught in the open, triumph soon turned to disaster for the Turks when the British navy opened fire and decimated them. In the end, they were forced to pull back and dug in again to re-establish the front lines.

CHAPTER TWELVE

The Turks

Far from proving the brittle enemy that Churchill imagined, the Turkish soldiers defending Gallipoli fought with tenacity and ferocity. In doing so they were sustained by their families and their religion.

There was scarcely a Turkish family that was untouched by death or injury and many of the front-line soldiers' families lived on the farms on the Peninsula or nearby and continued to supply them with food and clothing and encouraged them to fight to protect their loved-ones.

Turkey was a secular country but the soldiers' underlying religious beliefs were Islamic. They believed that the spirit of any Turkish soldier killed on the battleground would go directly to paradise as a martyr.

As Turkish historian, Ali Efe, explains, the soldiers were also sustained by two old sayings:

> 'One, it is the responsibility of any man, if he is a man, to sacrifice his own life to defend

AWM AO2598

Turkish soldiers of the 125th Regiment in their trenches.

his own family members. And two, if a man is
trying to defend his own wife, his own family,
he'll be two times stronger than normal.'

In addition, the Turkish defenders were mainly
farmers or country villagers, and were used to hard,
physical work and accustomed to living off the land – a
land they knew intimately.

As the days and weeks wore on, respect between
the Turks and the Anzacs for each others' bravery and
tenacity grew. Small but significant events illustrated
the changes in the soldiers' attitudes. Some Turkish
defenders around Quinn's Post tasted chocolate for
the first time when Anzacs threw some of their rations
instead of grenades. The Turks reciprocated with
tomatoes and apples. One day a white handkerchief tied
to a bayonet appeared in the Turkish lines. A small boy
dashed out unhindered and ran to the Anzac trenches,
dropped some bags and ran back. When the Anzacs
opened the bags, they found fine-cut tobacco with a
note saying, 'I tobacco ... you papier every day, every day.'

The Anzacs responded in kind. They scrounged all the
paper they could – old letters, newspapers, some 'rollies'
(cigarette papers) – and tossed them over. For a brief
moment amid the bloodshed, there was an unofficial
ceasefire as both sides contentedly puffed away.

꙰

Over the ensuing months the casualty rate dropped as the fighting settled into a dull daily routine, broken only by the occasional sortie. By and large, the two sides kept to their sophisticated networks of trenches and tunnels, still within touching distance, but were increasingly aware of the futility of the situation.

By mid-November, many combatants had been in continuous action for more than six months.

In the early days of the conflict, both sides rained grenades at other, but over time, their unreliability and the damage done to the throwing side (if the grenades were caught and returned) took its inevitable toll. As the campaign wore on, the frequency of grenade throwing decreased. Too many soldiers were being killed or maimed. In the end, both sides stopped throwing them altogether.

Both the Turkish and Allied soldiers knew the time had come to call it quits, but their commanders, as always, were less decisive.

CHAPTER THIRTEEN

Fading Glory

General Hamilton asked London for additional troops
– 45,000 to bring his existing force up to strength,
and an extra 50,000 to give him the numbers over
the Turks – but by now he'd lost High Command's
confidence.

So had General Stopford, the British commander
who had been so indecisive at the Suvla landings. He
was replaced by Major-General Beauvoir de Lisle, who
was despised by most as a bully. Other leaders were
shuffled out too but the horse had bolted. De Lisle
tried to energise the situation by attacking Scimitar
Hill and Hill 60, south of Suvla.

Scimitar Hill had changed hands four times. The
Turks eventually reclaimed it after inflicting another
5000 casualties on the British, including the loss
of three VC winners from the Boer War, without
conceding a metre of territory.

At Hill 60, de Lisle threw a mixture of Anzacs, the
29th Indian Brigade and three British battalions at the

deeply entrenched Turkish defences. Most of these units went in down on numbers, under-equipped and still reeling from the August Offensive. The fighting was furious and deadly and the Australian 9th Light Horse Brigade was badly hit. They blundered into a Turkish stronghold and lost their commander, two majors and a captain and almost all their troops.

The next day the 10th Light Horse Brigade recaptured the position and fought standing on the bodies of their dead mates. One soldier of the 10th, Lieutenant Hugo 'Jim' Throssell from Western Australia, was inspirational in defending the position against a series of ferocious Turkish counter-attacks. Throssell had already survived the trauma of The Nek where he'd charged in the fourth line. He and a handful of his mates on the left flank had miraculously survived by finding cover in a hollow under the muzzles of the Turkish machine guns. At Hill 60 he led the second wave of the attack that captured part of the Turkish trench. Despite being shot through the shoulder and neck, he and a few of his men held off counter-attacks against vastly superior numbers. He recalls:

> 'We just blazed away until the rifles grew red-
> hot and the chocks jammed and then picked
> up the rifles the killed men had left. When

Captain Hugo Vivien Hope Throssell VC of the 10th Australian Light
Horse Regiment.

we were wondering how long we could stand
against such numbers the Turks turned and
fled.'

The fighting raged for six hours, during which time
Throssell picked up several enemy grenades and
returned them before they exploded. He won the only
Victoria Cross awarded to the Australian Light Horse
Brigade at Gallipoli.

Hill 60 was also disastrous for the New Zealand
Mounted Rifles who went into battle with only 700
men out of their original 2000. At the end of it, only
half of these had survived and many were wounded.

Yet again, the fighting at Hill 60 ended in stalemate.
Indeed, the whole campaign was by now bogged down
and morale was at rock bottom.

The massive numbers of Allied casualties had
overwhelmed both the evacuation system and the
medical staff on the Peninsula and on the island of
Lemnos. Many wounded soldiers died before they
could be evacuated – either on the beaches waiting for
a boat, or during the long journey to hospital. As the
number of wounded grew, groups were sent to Egypt
and, later, to England for treatment.

The weather began to add to Hamilton's problems. The first of a series of severe storms heralded the arrival of winter in early October. Anzac Cove was hit heavily and the water supply was disrupted.

Around mid-October, Lord Kitchener brought up the notion of withdrawing the force from the Peninsula with Hamilton. Hamilton replied that it was 'unthinkable'.

The final straw was the intervention of Australian journalist Keith Murdoch (father of Rupert) who visited the battlefield. He had been sent to check on the mail service and to subsequently run the cable office from London. But he had many high-level political connections and many believe he also had an unofficial brief from the Australian Government to check on the position at Gallipoli.

Murdoch concluded the campaign was irreparably lost and that the Australian troops were being badly misused by their British commanders. He later met with the disaffected British war correspondent, Ellis Ashmead-Bartlett, on the island of Imbros, who supported his views.

Murdoch agreed to take a letter from Ashmead-Bartlett to the British Prime Minister Herbert Asquith in London. In it, he castigated the campaign and its leadership. But General Hamilton learned of the letter, had Murdoch's ship intercepted in Marseilles and confiscated it.

An incensed Murdoch met with politicians in London and immediately wrote a 17-page indictment against the campaign and its leaders. Although exaggerated – he called the campaign 'undoubtedly one of the most terrible chapters in our history' – Murdoch's letter contained many home truths and was circulated in British political circles, including the War Cabinet.

Hamilton tried to defend himself but by mid-October he had been relieved of his post and Birdwood was given temporary command pending the arrival of the new man, General Sir Charles Monro.

Monro showed the decisiveness that had been missing for so long. After touring the positions, he recommended evacuation, noting that he feared losses in doing so could reach 40 per cent. High Command was unimpressed and ordered Lord Kitchener to make a personal evaluation on the spot.

Winter was setting in on the Peninsula when Lord Kitchener arrived on 1 November 1915. At first, he was inclined to start a new front at Bulair but he soon recognised that evacuation was the only sensible course of action. The prospects of a breakout were negligible and there were more than 20,000 sick and wounded soldiers in hospitals on Lemnos and in Egypt.

AWM G01265

Winter at Gallipoli near Lone Pine.

Lord Kitchener ordered Birdwood to prepare a plan to implement an evacuation. As winter worsened, the plan gained in urgency. In late November the worst blizzard in 40 years hit the Peninsula, covering it with snow, sleet and rainstorms. Many men reported frostbite and 200 died from exposure at Suvla.

In addition, word was coming through that the Turkish defences were being reinforced with howitzers from Germany.

The order to start the evacuation was given on 8 December with the final pullout of Anzac Cove and Suvla to be completed by 20 December.

Under a blanket of secrecy, the plan was developed, largely by Brigadier-General Brudenell White. The central theme was a gradual withdrawal of troops under cover of darkness. Although the men were told some were simply being given a break from the frontline, many sensed a major change in the wind.

A series of ploys or 'stunts' were implemented to fool the Turks. One was the 'silent' stunt where the troops stopped firing for periods of half an hour to an hour to accustom the defenders to periods of inactivity. Another was the practice of sending out empty boats in daylight, and returning them later with apparent new reinforcements. These troops would be sent out again at night. Dummy soldiers, made from uniforms stuffed with straw, were distributed around crucial areas. The most famous stunt was the decoy rifle, devised by young Victorian Lance Corporal William Scurry. Rifles were set up against the sand bags and fired using water dripping from one tin to another that was wired so it pulled the trigger when it was full.

The animals were either evacuated or shot, and ammunition and stores were disposed of at night in the sea.

AWM G01291

Delayed action decoy rifle, invented by Lance Corporal William Charles Scurry (later Captain WC Scurry, MC, DCM) of the 7th Battalion, AIF.

The final stages of the evacuation required detailed planning and timing, with soldiers wrapping cloth over their boots to muffle their movements.

Many of the departing Allies left presents and notes for their enemy, wishing them good luck. Others set up booby traps. Hamilton had ordered a tunnel to be dug under Russell's Top, near The Nek. It was filled with a large store of explosives that were detonated by the last men out. The explosions killed at least 70 Turks. They anticipated an attack and kept up rapid fire and bombardment for some time at the deserted

AWM A05297

Five Turkish officers watch the Allied ships withdrawing from the Gallipoli Peninsula.

Anzac positions. Later, many Turks viewed the final gesture bitterly.

The evacuation was carried out successfully, with no deaths and just a few minor injuries. Keen to find positive aspects from the disastrous campaign, the Allies point to it with the same pride they later reserved for Dunkirk. But the Turks had a different view: they knew that their enemy was showing signs of withdrawing and, even though the fighting was far from over, victory was about to be theirs.

On 7 January 1916, von Sanders launched a massive attack against the British at Gully Spur, down from Y Beach. The attack was preceded by a huge artillery bombardment but the British troops fought with great determination in the knowledge that evacuation was imminent, and inflicted heavy losses on the Turks. The second wave of the Turkish attack refused to charge. The true state of the campaign was now evident to all.

Over the next two nights the British completed the evacuation of the Peninsula. They left behind a huge store of weapons and stores ... and thousands of their dead comrades.

CHAPTER FOURTEEN

A Special Aura

Looking back, the statistics clearly reveal the futility of the Gallipoli campaign. The original plan was to take the Peninsula in 11 days. It dragged out to 240 days and ended in defeat. The Anzacs penetrated a mere 1.2 kilometres inland from their landings – Lone Pine marks the point of farthest advance. The British reached 5.5 kilometres inland at Cape Helles and 3.2 kilometres at Suvla Bay. In 240 days they captured less than 1 per cent of the Peninsula.

During the campaign an extra 420,000 Allied troops joined the original 80,000-strong invasion force. The Turks more than matched this number. Between 50,000 and 60,000 Australian troops and 8500 New Zealanders served on Gallipoli. By the end, the Turks had suffered about 250,000 casualties (with more than 86,000 killed). Some sources put this figure much higher, with up to 150,000 deaths. The Allies' casualty list totalled around 140,000 (44,000 killed).

LISA COTTON

Tombstones at The Nek
where the flower of the
Light Horse fell.

Some 8700 Australian soldiers were killed and a
further 19,400 were wounded or sick, while the New
Zealanders lost 2700 men and 4700 were sick or
wounded.

❧

In spite of the fierceness of the fighting, the Gallipoli
conflict has brought Australia and New Zealand closer
to Turkey. As early as 1951, just two years after Turkish
and Australian forces fought together in the Korean
War, this time as allies, they co-celebrated Anzac Day.

Today the Victorian RSL has a Turkish sub-branch that marches in the Anzac Day Parade.

Drawn by the spirit of Anzac, each year the sacred sands of the Gallipoli Peninsula attract Australians and New Zealanders in ever growing numbers. They come in search of their national roots and to pay homage to those brave young men who shed their blood and helped to establish our national identities.

The Anzac spirit forms the bedrock of the Australian and New Zealand national characters. It was forged when soldiers from both nations instinctively banded

AWM P01251.001

Anzacs enjoy a smoko as they rest under cover. Their .303 rifles are stacked within reach.

together and developed a mateship that grew into something greater than the shared experiences of brothers-in-arms.

The mateship came from within and extended outward. It formed a cocoon that enveloped the young soldiers and made their existence on Gallipoli bearable. The unconditional support created teamwork that produced a force far greater than its individual components; it often meant the difference between life and death.

A visit to Gallipoli is a pilgrimage to the land where that spirit was first displayed to the world. It's a visit that brings great rewards.

On the dull sands at Anzac Cove, on the hallowed heights at Lone Pine or The Nek, in the ravines and gullies, along the ridges at Quinn's Post, on the coasts at Suvla and Helles, you can feel the spirits of the young men who died. Standing near the concrete remains of Watson's Pier, you can look up at the Sphinx and the foreboding heights that faced the young Anzacs when they landed. You can see where they swam during their brief breaks from the tensions of the front lines. You can imagine the constant danger of shelling from the Turkish artillery raining death on them from their hidden emplacements behind the high ground.

LISA COTTON

Anzac Cove, showing the narrow beachhead and the hills rising
immediately behind it.

LISA COTTON

The author taking notes at Lone Pine.

On the headland at the northern end of the beach, Ari Burnu Cemetery holds the remains of some of the first casualties of the campaign. Resting there are men of the 8th and 10th Light Horse Regiments – the heroes of The Nek. Here you'll find the wonderful memorial where Turkey has honoured the Anzacs, soldiers of two countries, that came to invade it.

Clambering up through the scrub to Plugge's Plateau, you can look through the eyes of the young Allied troops as the terrible realities of war first struck home. Imagine the feelings that coursed through them as they saw mates dying and wounded and faced their fears and somehow found the courage to charge on through the storm of deadly shrapnel and bullets that raged around them.

On the high ground you can see the trenches from both sides, just as they were — some separated by a single roadway, so close you could almost hear each others' heartbeats.

Even in the heavy silence at Lone Pine, you can still hear the long-gone echoes of the guns and bombs and screams as men fought to the death. Despite the brutal scenes played out here, there is a tranquillity now — as though the tortured souls who lie here have finally found peace in each others' embrace.

That the Turkish people have dedicated the battlefields as a sacred memorial brings nobility to the countless sacrifices made.

It's easy to understand the feelings of Charles Bean, who looked back from the ship as the Anzacs left the fateful shore behind them:

'By dawn on December 20th Anzac had faded into a dim blue line lost amid other hills on the horizon as the ships took their human freight to Imbros, Lemnos and Egypt. But Anzac stood, and still stands, for reckless valour in a good cause, for enterprise, resourcefulness, fidelity, comradeship, and endurance that will never own defeat.'

The British commander at Gallipoli, General Sir Ian Hamilton, best summed it up: 'Before the war, who had ever heard of Anzac? Hereafter, who will ever forget it?'

AWM A05534

The Anzac spirit is evident in the faces of these men at Quinn's Post.

World War I 1914–18

OVERALL LOSSES

CENTRAL POWERS (GERMANY/AUSTRIA/TURKEY/BULGARIA)

Mobilized	Killed	Wounded	Missing	Total	% casualties
22.8m	3.3m	8.3m	3.6m	15m	67%

ALLIED POWERS (RUSSIA/BRITAIN/AUSTRALIA/NZ/CANADA/ITALY/
USA/JAPAN/ROMANIA/SERBIA/BELGIUM

Mobilized	Killed	Wounded	Missing	Total	% casualties
42 m	5m	13m	4m	22m	52%

AUSTRALIANS

Mobilized	Killed	Wounded		Total	% casualties
330,000	59,000	152,000		211,000	64%

NEW ZEALANDERS

Mobilized	Killed	Wounded		Total	% casualties
110,000	18,000	55,000		73,000	66%

CASUALTIES

GALLIPOLI CAMPAIGN

	Killed in Action	Wounded	Total
Turkey	86,692	164,000	250,690
Britain	21,255	52,230	73,485
France	9798	17,000 (est)	26,798
Australia	8709	19,441	28,150
New Zealand	2701	4852	7553
India	1358	3421	4779
Newfoundland	49	93	142
Total Allies	44,072	97,037	141,109

DATELINE WORLD WAR I

28 JUNE 1914   Archduke Franz Ferdinand, heir to the Emperor of Austria–Hungary, and his wife, are assassinated by a Serbian nationalist named Gavrilo Princip while in Sarajevo, the capital of Bosnia, a former Ottoman Turkish province that had been occupied by Austria in 1878.

Serbia was described then as an aggressive, backward and domestically violent Christian kingdom that had won its independence from the Muslim Ottoman Empire after centuries of rebellion. They were defeated by the Turks in 1839, ironically on 28 June, and they regard this as the start of their history of foreign oppression.

The Numbers

4 JULY 1914	Austria decides war on Serbia is the only acceptable response. It demands guarantees of Serbia's future conduct under treat of military action.
5 JULY 1914	Kaiser Wilhelm II of Germany advises Austria's Emperor Franz Josef he can 'rely on Germany's full support'. Then he goes on a three-week's holiday cruise in the Norwegian fjords.
23 JULY 1914	Austria delivers note to Serbia demanding that those responsible for the assassination be brought to justice and that Austro-Hungarian officials be permitted to supervise the investigations.
25 JULY 1914	The Serbians were on the verge of capitulating when they heard from their Ambassador at the Russian Tsar's country palace that the Tsar was prepared to support them and that he had given a preliminary signal for mobilising his army. They replied with an indecisive note.
28 JULY 1914	Austria–Hungary declares war on Serbia.
30 JULY 1914	Russia mobilises.
31 JULY 1914	Germany demands reversal of Russian mobilisation and that France indicates it will remain neutral otherwise Germany will mobilise itself.
2 AUG 1914	France mobilises.

2 AUG 1914	Germany demands Belgium give it access to its territory for actions against France or be treated as an enemy itself.
4 AUG 1914	Britain demands Germany stop military operations against Belgium by midnight. Nor response received so Britain, France and Russia were officially at war with Germany.

WESTERN FRONT

4 AUG 1914	German forces cross the Belgian frontier and begin attacking Belgian civilians as enemy combatants.
4 AUG 1914	Australia declares war on Germany, following Britain's lead.
7 AUG 1914	France seizes Mulhouse in Alsace.
10 AUG 1914	Recruitment starts for the AIF (aiming at raising an expeditionary force of 200,000. RAN is placed under Admiralty control.
14 AUG 1914	Lorraine offensive begins as France advances.
18 AUG 1914	USA declares itself neutral.
20 AUG 1914	German counter-attacks force French back.
22 AUG 1914	BEF arrives at Mons-Conde Canal and deploys across a front of 32 kms.

24 AUG 1914	BEF and French forces begin the Great Retreat over a fortnight back to the outskirts of Paris.
4 SEPT 1914	Battle of the Marne begins. (The Marne River served as a natural barrier between the advancing Germans and Paris.)
9 SEPT 1914	German army had overreached itself and was ordered back to positions along the Aisne and its tributaries.
10 SEPT 1914	German Commander, General Molte, orders his troops: 'The lines so reached will be fortified and defended.' This was the start of trench warfare. The days of open warfare were finished.
11 SEPT 1914	Australian Naval and Military expeditionary force attacks German New Guinea positions at Rabaul.
10 OCT– 22 NOV 1914	First Battle of Ypres. By this stage, in less than four months' fighting, the French incur 500,000 casualties, including 300,000 killed (45,000 under 20, 90,000 between 20–24, 70,000 between 25–29) out of a male population of 20 million. Germany, with a male population of 32 million, had lost 240,000; Belgium out 1.8 million males, had lost 30,000. Britain lost about 30,000. The front line is a continuous line of trenches, running 760 kilometres from the North Sea to the mountains of Switzerland.

EASTERN FRONT

15 AUG 1914	First Russian Army advances into East Prussia to assist France by diverting German attention.
18 AUG 1914	Russia invades Eastern Galicia, makes fast progress.
20 AUG 1914	Second Russian Army advances into East Prussia.
23 AUG 1914	Hindenburg and Ludendorff given command of the German Eastern Front.
26–30 AUG 1914	Battle of Tannenberg becomes a decisive victory for the Germans after they surround and defeat both Russian armies, taking 92,000 prisoners and annihilating half of the Russian 2nd Army. The victory reversed Germany's war plan. Originally, it intended to drive for victory in the west while holding on their eastern front. After Tannenberg, it felt no real threat from the east.
7 SEPT 1914	First Battle of the Masurian Lakes begins. German forces victorious again.
4 OCT 1914	Germany and Austria–Hungary jointly invade Russia.
1 NOV 1914	First AIF convoy sails from Albany for Egypt.
2 NOV 1914	Russia declares war on Turkey.

The Numbers

5 NOV 1914	Turkey joins the Central Powers; Britain and France declare war on her.
9 NOV 1914	HMAS *Sydney* destroys the German cruiser SMS *Emden*, forcing her shore on Cocos Island.
4 DEC 1914	First AIF reaches Egypt and begins training at Mena Camp.
21 DEC 1914	Germany launches its first air raids on Britain.
25 DEC 1914	Troops share an unofficial Christmas Truce in the Western Front trenches.
31 JAN 1915	Germany first uses poison gas at Bolimow in Poland.
4 FEB 1915	Germany declares submarine blockade of Britain. All ships are considered targets and unrestricted submarine warfare begins.
7–21 FEB 1915	Second Battle of the Masurian Lakes sees no victor.
11 MAR 1915	Britain bans all 'neutral' parties from trading with Germany.
11–13 MAR 1915	Battle of Neuve-Chapelle on western Front begins.
18 MAR 1915	Allied ships try unsuccessfully to force the Dardanelles.

22 APR– 25 MAY 1915	Second Battle of Ypres begins and Britain suffers three times the casualties of Germany.
25 APR 1915	Gallipoli landings begin.
26 APR 1915	The Treaty of London is signed and Italy joins the Entente.
22 APR 1915	Germans first use poison gas on the Western Front on Canadians at Ypres.
2–13 MAY 1915	The Germans push back the Russians in the battle of Gorlice-Tarnow.
7 MAY 1915	The *Lusitania* is sunk by a German submarine; casualties include 124 Americans passengers.
23 JUNE– 8 JULY 1915	First Battle of Isonzo occurs where Italian troops attack fortified Austrian positions along an 80km front.
13–15 JULY	The German 'Triple Offensive' begins, aiming to destroy the Russian army.
22 JULY 1915	The Second Great Retreat begins as Russian forces pull back out of Poland, then part of Russia, taking machinery and equipment with them.
1 SEPT 1915	After American outrage, Germany officially stops sinking passenger vessels without warning.
5 SEPT 1915	Tsar Nicholas II makes himself Russian Commander-in-Chief.

12 SEPT 1915	Following the failure of the Austrian 'Black Yellow' offensive on the Eastern Front, Germany takes over ultimate control of Austro-Hungarian forces.
21 SEPT– 6 NOV 1915	The Allies begin the battles of Champagne, Second Artois and Loos but have little success.
23 NOV 1915	German, Austro-Hungarian and Bulgarian forces push the Serbian army into exile; Serbia falls.
10 DEC 1915	The Allies slowly begin withdrawing from Gallipoli. They complete the task by 9 January 1916.

Bibliography

Arthur, Max, *Symbol of Courage: the men behind the medal*, Pan Books, London, 2005

Askin, Mustafa, Gallipoli: A Turning Point, Keskin Color, Canakkale, 2001

Bean, C.E.W., *Anzac to Amiens*, Australian War Memorial, Canberra, 1983

Bean, C.E.W., *The Official History of Australia in the War of 1914-1918*, Australian War Memorial, Canberra, 1933

Bell, A.D., *An Anzac's War Diary: The Story of Sergeant Richardson*, Rigby, Sydney, 1981

Broadbent, Harvey, *Gallipoli: the Fatal Shore*, Penguin Viking, Melbourne, 2005

Denning, Roy & Lorna, *Anzac Digger: An Engineer in Gallipoli & France*, Australian Military History Publications, Sydney, 2004

Denton, Kit, *Gallipoli Illustrated*, Rigby, Sydney, 1981

Fasih, Mehmet, *Gallipoli 1915: Bloody Ridge (Lone Pine) Diary*, Denizler Kitabevi, Istanbul, 1997

Fromkin, David, *A Peace to End All Peace: The Fall of the Ottoman Empire and the Creation of the Middle East*, Phoenix Press, London, 2004

Haynes, Jim, *Cobbers: Stories of Gallipoli 1915*, ABC Books, Sydney, 2005

Keegan, John, *The First World War*, Pimlico, London, 2002

King, Jonathan, & Bowers, Michael, *Gallipoli: Untold Stories from War Correspondent Charles Bean and front-line Anzacs*, Doubleday, Sydney, 2005

Kyle, Roy, *An Anzac's Story*, Penguin Books, Melbourne, 2003

Lindsay, Patrick, *The Spirit of The Digger ... Then & Now*, Macmillan, Sydney, 2003

Malthus, Cecil, *Anzac: A Retrospect*, Reed, Auckland, 2002

Miller, William Ian, *The Mystery of Courage*, Harvard University Press, Cambridge, Massachusetts, 2000

Pedersen, P.A., *Images of Gallipoli: Photographs from the collection of Ross J Bastiaan*, Oxford University Press Australia, Melbourne, 1988

Pelvin, Richard, *Anzac: An Illustrated History 1914-1918*, Hardie Grant Books, 2004

Reid, Richard, *Gallipoli 1915*, ABC Books, Sydney, 2002

Snelling, Stephen, *VCs of The First War: Gallipoli*, Wrens Park Publishing, London, 1995

Stanley, Peter, *Quinn's Post: Anzac Gallipoli*, Allen & Unwin, Sydney, 2005

Staunton, Anthony, *Victoria Cross: Australia's Finest and the Battles they Fought*, Hardie Grant Books, Melbourne, 2005

Steel, Nigel, & Hart, Peter, Defeat at Gallipoli, Pan, London, 2002

Stevenson, David, *1914-1918: The History of the First World War*, Allen Lane, London, 2004

Travers, Tim, *Gallipoli 1915*, Tempus, London, 2001

Williams, John F, *Anzacs, the Media and the Great War*, UNSW Press, Sydney, 1999